Scots on Scotch
MADE IN SCOTLAND

Scots on Scotch

The Book of Whisky

Edited by Phillip Hills

MAINSTREAM PUBLISHING

EDINBURGH AND LONDON

First published in Great Britain 1991 by
MAINSTREAM PUBLISHING (EDINBURGH) LTD
7 Albany Street
Edinburgh EH1 3UG

ISBN 1 84018 608 9

This edition, 2002

A catalogue record for this book is available from the British Library

Typeset in Stone

Printed in Great Britain by
Cox & Wyman Ltd

Acknowledgement of the help
given by the following:

Bells Whisky plc
Dr Morgan of United Distillers' Archives
Gordon McIntosh and the Keepers of the Quaich
Murray and Barbara Grigor

CONTENTS

PREFACE TO THE 2002 EDITION

When, more than ten years ago, this work was projected, it was with a purpose. The book was intended to set down a marker for Scotland and her whisky, saying, "This is where we are now and this is how we got here." I felt there was a need for such a marker because, while things were getting much better as regards Scotch whisky, I could see that the forces of unreason were still abroad in the land.

A lot has happened in those ten years as regards Scotch whisky. We have seen malt whiskies rise from a minority taste in a small, poor nation to become internationally recognised as the connoisseur's spirit par excellence. The position once held by fine cognacs and armagnacs is now occupied by malt Scotch. The whisky which once was drunk from tumblers of ice is now accorded due respect and savoured from nosing glasses. No posh hotel can afford not to have a malt bar: some have bottles displayed like icons behind lamplit glass. The mere nosing of malt has become a popular leisure activity in the USA and in many other places.

In some ways the rise of malt whisky at the end of the 20th century – in terms of market prominence if not in terms of volume – parallels the rise of blended whisky in the last decade of the 19th. Where the two things differ is in the position which Scotland has played. In the 19th century, Scotland was firmly part of the great British

Empire. She was the first and closest colony and her products were regarded in the same way as those of other, more distant colonies: as tributes to the only culture which really mattered. The Victorian gentlemen who drank the whisky knew little about Scotland, and what they did know was restricted to a fabricated identity which bore as much similarity to the real thing as their whisky did to a prime malt. The rise of malt whiskies in the 1990s, by contrast, was an integral part of a renaissance of the Scottish people, who, reclaiming their true history, reclaimed also the finest form of their national drink. The same decade saw the re-establishment of the Scottish Parliament and the revival of malt whisky. Some of the people whom I asked for contributions to this book contributed also to the cultural revival which produced both. Hamish Henderson, the decent man, died the day before I wrote these words. He, more than anyone else, brought to the notice of the world the sheer brilliance of the song-culture of the ordinary people of Scotland. He also liked his glass of malt and was present at the first, absurd meeting of what became the Scotch Malt Whisky Society's tasting committee. Freedom and whisky gang indeed thegither.

The Scotch whisky industry was slow to apprehend the opportunity created by the revival of interest in malt whiskies. But, having grasped the idea, its performance has been impressive. Malts are now marketed wherever people drink whisky and the range of product available would have brought joy to the heart of Norman MacCaig, who gave me permission to publish his 'Ballade of Good Whisky', as well as to Hugh MacDiarmid, to whom it was addressed. Whether they would have been so happy about the manner in which some of those malts are sold is another matter. For along with the internationalisation of malt whiskies has gone, inevitably, the internationalisation of their marketing. For the people who sell the stuff, what matters most is, naturally, selling as much of it as possible. To that end they employ whatever description of the whisky they think will most appeal to the people they wish to sell it to. As a result, the association between any authentically Scottish culture and the whisky is inevitably broken. We can see this most clearly in some parts of North America, where the malt whisky aficionado knows little of Scotland and what he does know consists only of kilts and tartans. What is more, he sees whisky as only one among the many tributes paid by quasi-colonised countries to the great American imperium. So we seem to be getting back to where we started. The changes in the Scotch whisky industry over the last ten years haven't helped. The trend has been towards ever-greater conglomeration of ownership of whisky brands and distilleries by supra-national corporations. In the brands, portfolios of such organisations, Scotch whisky is only one among many different types of product. It is not therefore to be expected that the folk who sell the stuff will give much thought to its cultural associations.

However it's not all one-way, and the last few years have seen a countervailing trend. Some of the most successful companies have remained Scottish in their ownership, their staff and in the values with which they promote their product. One thinks of Edrington, Highland Distillers, and William Grant & Sons. Or of the Whyte & Mackay directors who bought the company out from American Brands and now run it as Kindall, a Scottish company. Or of Bruichladdich, which after decades of neglect is now being run from Scotland – and at long last making one of the greatest malts available to the world.

With any luck, the marker won't be needed. Whether it is or not, most of the stuff in the book will still be worth perusing for its own sake. Re-reading it, I have been pleasantly surprised at how little it has dated. It provides a picture of its time and of times before, of a small nation and its national drink, and how the two have gone together in the pursuit of that liberty which no man yields but with his life.

Phillip Hills

If I had to say why this book came to be written, I suppose I would say that it was the outcome of astonishment, and maybe indignation. Some years ago, a few friends and I set up an organisation which we called the Scotch Malt Whisky Society. Its object, of which more in due course, was to make generally available the malt whisky which for some time we had enjoyed as a private indulgence. Our little enterprise proved successful, which was surprising to quite a few folk who knew a lot more about what we were trying to do than we did, and who had predicted doom. It wasn't surprising to us, or at least not at first, for we were sure the time was ripe for what we planned to do. Surprise came later, as we learned something about what we had done: surprise that it should have been possible – or necessary – for us to do it at all.

I guess the first thing to do is to tell you what we did, and then try to explain why it was surprising. I have told the story more than once, so those who have heard it before should skip the next page or two.

Malt whisky was unknown in the society in which I grew up, that is, industrial Lowland Scotland of the 1950s. Whisky meant Bell's or Haig, and you drank it with a pint of export ale. Called a half and a nip, or a hauf an' a hauf, the whisky prepared the palate for the beer and the latter whetted the appetite for the former, a deadly combination. In neither case did it much matter what the stuff tasted like. I don't care for either and, despite applying myself assiduously, found it hard to acquire a taste for one or the other.

Beer drinking was the badge and guarantee of adult masculinity, and the beer was sweet, gassy and cold. It was some years before I discovered one that was palatable – what Dylan Thomas called flat, warm, bitter Welsh beer, though in this case it was English – and I recall being derided by my mates for entertaining the stuff. Why, you could drink half a gallon of it and not get pissed! It was, of course, what later came to be called real ale. The only approximation I could find in the Edinburgh of the 1960s was beer brewed by Campbell, Hope and King. It was to be had in a pub called the Hole i' the Wa'. Shortly after, both brewery and pub were bought by one of the bigger, more modern brewers who made the gassy stuff and both were demolished. There was muttering in a few taverns, but no protest.

Now by this time you may be asking why I write about my dolorous experiences with beer, in a book which is supposed to be about whisky. There are two reasons. Firstly, you have to be able to make good beer to make good whisky, for whisky is distilled beer, as brandy is distilled wine. Scotland's pre-eminence in whisky has been due not only to her distillers, but to the skill of her brewers. (The brewer is as important a person in any distillery as the stillman.) Secondly, as this is not so well known, Edinburgh was once more famous for beer than for whisky; the Munich rather than the Athens of the North, as far as beer drinkers were concerned. Yet the condition of Scottish society was such that it was possible, over the first half of the 20th century, progressively to change the quality of the beer to a point where a great ale could simply be removed in the interests of improved profitability in the accounts of some bureaucratic corporation and nobody said a thing. The people who were in charge either didn't know good beer from bad, or didn't care. Probably the former, for those who controlled brewery companies didn't drink beer, which had always been the preserve of the lower orders.

Whisky was different. All Scots drank whisky, or were supposed to. The whisky they drank was blended whisky. Few asked where it came from or how it was made. Despite the prominence of whisky in the national identity, it was commonplace for Scots to know nothing of its manufacture, and less of the process of maturation. This was the *vin du pays*, and the parallel which keeps coming to mind is with French or Italian wine production. I find it difficult to believe that French kids in a wine-growing area can grow up, study six years of the physical and biological sciences in secondary school and go to university, knowing as little of the fundamentals of wine production as we did about whisky.

'Blended' had a fine, eulogistic ring to it, suggestive of a synthesis in which the whisky was greater than the sum of its part. As late as the 1960s, malt whisky simply did not figure in the general consciousness. It was something for enthusiasts who, by and large, weren't taken seriously. No wonder, for they were proposing something which was alien to popular psychology, namely that you should seriously consider what your whisky tasted like.

In the course of preparing this book, we collected a vast number of advertising images of whisky. There are very few that make any mention of taste. As Colin McArthur points out later, they mention just about everything else you can think of, from elephants to poltergeists, but they are distinctly coy about taste. Maybe they thought that to do so would be a bit tasteless. Whisky – which meant blended whisky – was, and is, sold by reference to symbols and self-conceptions, prejudices and beliefs of the most bizarre sort. Rarely is there any mention, direct or indirect, of what the stuff tastes like. It is clear that from a very early date, the distillers had decided that whisky should be advertised by brand image rather than on the basis of any gustatory qualities. The only references to taste are indirect. Apart from a few mentions of smoothness, the sole indicator of quality is age. Whiskies are described as being old, very old and mature, but at no point is the public informed of the implications. It is presumed that age is a sufficient condition of maturity and, since other criteria are absent, there is an implication that age alone is a guarantee of quality in the liquor. That this is far from being the case, we were to discover.

I took to malt whisky as I had done to decent beer, and for the same reason. It was pretty rare stuff in the 1960s. There were a few pubs in Edinburgh where you could call up a malt, and some, very few, which stocked half a dozen. Outside Scotland malt whisky was virtually unknown, or if it was known, the folk who knew it weren't known to me, which I admit is not quite the same thing. As the 1970s progressed, so did single malt whiskies, as they then came to be called, and by the end of the 1970s, they were reasonably common in the South. This was a change which was purely demand-led; the distillers, with a very few, laudable exceptions, were slow indeed to discern a potential market. The demand originated in Scotland, where it grew in the later 1960s. By the early 1980s, malts had become established as whisky for the cognoscenti, and foreign markets developed as people came to realise that this was a product quite different from the Scotch whisky to which they were accustomed.

In the 1970s it was – and still is – my practice to pay a visit once or twice a year to two old friends who have a small farm on the edge of the Howe of Alford, in rural Aberdeenshire. Their next-door neighbour ran a large herd of Herefords, was in affluent circumstances and had a taste for fine malt whisky and political dispute, in about equal measure. Stan had little opportunity to indulge the latter, but the former he kept alive by once a year taking his old Land Rover (he was a frugal man) over the hill to Speyside, to Ballindalloch, where he bought a quarter cask of Glenfarclas from George Grant. He paid cash and he kept the cask by his fireside, with a spigot in it, from which he drew his drams, straight from wood to glass.

Whenever I visited Denmill, Stan would learn about it and would turn up with a bottle of dark amber liquor for an evening of castigating socialism in any of its manifestations (which included virtually all social and economic legislation from Lloyd George onward) and exhorting me to breed a loon. (I have two daughters.) Stan affected to be unenlightened, or maybe he was just short of argument and made the most of what he could get. He did know a good dram, though, and his Glenfarclas was the finest thing of its sort I have ever met. Having come from the cask, it was at proof strength, and by the end of the evening Stan could barely walk home and I was falling off my chair.

The morning was remarkably clear. This was especially

gratifying for me, for I am sometimes immobilised for two days after such a bout, albeit on lesser liquor. I was so impressed with the whisky, which was far superior to any of the malts I had drunk, that I formed a syndicate of my friends in Edinburgh, and we bought a cask of Glenfarclas. I went up to Ballindalloch to collect it and we met in the lobby of my house and siphoned the contents off into gallon jars. There is a lot more to this story, but to cut it short, the syndicate was a great success. We tried casks of other whiskies and all were amazingly good. Members of the syndicate gave drams to their friends and the friends rang up to ask if they might become members of the syndicate. We doubled it in size, so that my lobby began to get quite crowded. The old Lagonda with trailer and two casks of whisky became quite a common sight on the A9.

Two things became apparent. One was that we couldn't go on increasing the size of the syndicate, for my lobby couldn't hold more than a given number of drunks clutching gallon jars of malt whisky. The other was that the whisky was actually better stuff – by which I mean precisely that we all liked its taste better – than the same malt out of a bottle.

I did some detective work with a view to ascertaining why the whisky tasted better than the malt of the same name from a proprietary bottle. It turned out that there were two main reasons. Firstly, casks of whisky vary greatly in type and quality, and the cask has a profound influence on the whisky that is matured in it. When bottling malt, the distillers put together the contents of many casks, some of which are necessarily not of the highest quality. (Credit here should be given to distillers such as Macallan and Glenfarclas, who for many years have matured their whiskies in very good casks indeed, but they are exceptional and most malt distillers still mature some of their product in indifferent wood.)

Secondly, we were taking the stuff straight from the cask, whereas almost all of those distillers who bottled malt at all, bottled it after subjecting it to a process called chill-filtering. This consists of refrigerating the spirit and then filtering it very finely, so as to ensure that the whisky in the bottle cannot go cloudy. The result is, by any standard, a very fine liquor, but it lacks some of the character of malt whisky taken, unfiltered, from a single cask. (I should say here that an exception to the rule, then as now, was Glenfarclas. John and George Grant bottle a cask-strength malt without chill-filtering.)

The syndicate members were unanimous that the syndicate whisky simply tasted better than any other malt they had drunk and that malts tasted a lot nicer than blends. So were a lot of their friends, who wanted to join the syndicate. So, in a spirit of pure, if bibulous, altruism, I considered how the undoubted benefits of syndicate membership might be spread more widely. The result was a scheme for an organisation to be called the Scotch Malt Whisky Society, which would be open to all, and which would make available to a wider public the whisky which the syndicate had enjoyed. It would be a limited company and each syndicate member would be a shareholder.

The history of the whisky industry is littered with failed attempts to set up independent marketing organisations, some of which have caused inconvenience and loss to the distillers, so the latter were understandably reluctant to countenance outsiders with daft ideas. There were legal impediments as well as apparently severe technical ones. Our problems were compounded by the fact that we really were amateurs and had few connections with the industry. I spoke to a number of professionals, outlining the scheme, and was invariably told that it couldn't work, often on the grounds that if it could have been done, somebody would have done it before. The technical objections were the most difficult to overcome, for they needed expert knowledge.

One of the syndicate members was an old pal of mine, John Ferguson. My first encounter with Ferguson had been 20 years before on the north face of Aonach Dubh in Glencoe, when Haston and I had nearly been killed by an avalanche Ferguson had started. Ferguson was a big, generous, easy-going guy, who would swim across the Firth of Lorne for an evening exercise; a mighty man with a timber axe or bottle, and a bonny singer. He was a member of a ruffianly Glasgow mountaineering club and hence of a sort of mafia of once wild but now ageing Scots mountaineers. It was this connection which enabled him to arrange a meeting, in the Horseshoe Bar in Glasgow, with one Russell Sharp, who was by way of being one of the whisky industry's technical experts. He is now the society's technical director and an essay by him on the effects of the cask in maturation follows. Russell said of course it couldn't be done but, if we did it, he would like to be part of it.

So, thus armed with technical expertise, we formed a company, hired some staff and got ourselves a building. The building was called The Vaults and was – is – the oldest commercial building in Scotland still used for anything like its original purpose. It is a four-storey wine warehouse, built some time before the 15th century by the abbots of Newbattle, bought in 1705 by John Thomson as a single-storey building and raised to its present height by his descendants, John and George Thomson, in 1785. It was still in use by J. & G. Thomson & Co., wine merchants, when I walked in off the street one day in 1981 and asked if I could buy it. I could and, with the help of a few friends, did.

We set about restoring the building, bought a few casks

of whisky, bottled them under our own label, told the would-be members of the whisky syndicate what we had done, and waited to see what would happen.

We were pretty clear about the sort of organisation we wanted to see. It was to be in the spirit of the original syndicate, that is cheerful, iconoclastic and a lot of fun. It had to make a profit sufficient to ensure it survived and gave a decent return, but it didn't have to make a fortune, and the cost of the stuff was to be kept down as far as possible, so that anybody who could afford to drink whisky could afford to join. We realised that if it worked, it would be the sort of organisation that would attract nobs and snobs and we wanted to make it quite clear that having been conceived in a socially ecumenical, democratic spirit of a sort that we like to associate with Scotland, it was to stay that way. And if the aim was not merely to maximise profit, we could eschew the mendacity which is the stuff of so much advertising. In fact we couldn't afford to advertise, so we made a virtue of necessity and decided not to, reasoning firstly that we were under no obligation to anybody to bring the stuff to them (we had after all gone to a lot of trouble to get it for ourselves) and secondly that if it was as good as we thought it was, the drinking public would find us.

It worked. They did. At the time of writing we have more than 12,000 members and our latest list of malt whiskies is without doubt the finest collection of distilled liquors to have been offered to the public in the history of this planet.

That, very roughly, is what we did. The surprising thing is that it should have been possible to do it. It was surprising, to say the least, that the finest product of the country's principal, and most characteristic, industry should not have been available to all. It was even more surprising that the greater part of that industry was not aware of the fact. How could this be?

Once I started to ask that question, others followed. We had discovered single-cask malts, but what about the folk who discovered malts in the first place, and what had the malts been doing that they needed to be discovered? What had the Scottish nation been doing that it had allowed its finest drink to disappear for generations? There was no shortage of people who would proclaim themselves guardians of our national heritage and culture. There were lots of people who spent a lot of their time dressing up in kilts and drinking whisky at swanky London dinners and Burns suppers and the like. Some of them were professional Scots. What had those guys been doing all this time? And more particularly, what had they been drinking?

Was it really possible that a whole nation had been completely ignorant of its own finest liquor? That the nation should have built its self-image around its national drink, and have been grossly deceived in that particular? It seems scarcely credible that that should have been the case, but undoubtedly it was, if you accept the premise that malt whisky by and large tastes better than grain whisky, which is the principal constituent of most blends. (I have yet to meet anyone who knows his stuff who seriously challenges this view.) What sort of nation could do such a thing?

The parallel with our old allies, the French, is one which keeps asserting itself in this context. I do not pretend that the analogy is an exact one, but it is persuasive. Imagine, if you will, a France in which the vineyards are mostly owned by a few companies and the directors of those companies have decided that their profits will be improved if the best and least of their wines are mixed together and sold as blended wines. It is a

France in which almost nobody protests about this, save a few of the small vineyard owners, who can be discounted, and the great wines of Burgundy and Bordeaux have been obscured to the point where few people even know that they exist. The middle and upper classes, who are the people who know about such things, the connoisseurs of fine wines, drink the blended wine and pronounce it the best there is. To be French is to be a member of the nation which produces French wine.

The absurdity of the notion is immediately apparent. Yet what is described is remarkably like what happened to Scotch whisky and Scotland about a hundred years ago. The pressing question then becomes: what sort of a nation was it that could allow such a thing to happen? Who was in charge, and why were they allowed to do it? Why was there not another rebellion, or a revolution, as there would have been in France had anyone offered such an insult to the national psyche?

It was with a view to answering, or at least addressing, some of these questions that this book was conceived. It seemed appropriate that, having been instrumental in the renaissance of malt whisky, the Society should ask some of its members to contribute to an understanding of what had happened. Most of the writers who follow know a lot more about the events described than I do, so I will merely try to outline what seems to have happened, leaving some of them to comment on an aspect of a national disruption as serious as any that has gone before; others to comment on Scotland and malt whisky as they are today or recently were. A new light on an auld licht.

By the third quarter of the 19th century, Scotland was well into the process of yielding most of the things which constituted an independent nation, exchanging them for tinsel icons of Scottishness. She was the closest and most willing colony in the British Empire. The successful merchants and manufacturers, who were making an awful lot of money out of the combination of Empire and industrial revolution, were the dominant social class and, like all emergent bourgeois, sought legitimacy in proximity to their betters. The Scottish aristocracy had for some time been culturally indistinguishable from their English counterparts. The thing to be was British, not Scots, for the dominant force in the world was Britain and things British were coming to be regarded with an awe and an admiration which it is difficult for us now to comprehend. (The approval of things American in the post-war years is a poor shadow.)

It was one of the great strengths of the British social system that it could accommodate a burgeoning industrial and mercantile bourgeoisie while maintaining the appearance of an immutably fixed social hierarchy. The process of legitimising wealth was then, as now, one of joining or approximating to a landed aristocracy. Whisky barons bought country estates just as yuppies buy Barbour jackets. Some of the most important Scots were among the most orthodox of conformists. Tommy Dewar, returning from one of his foreign trips, wrote how wonderful it was to come back to dear old London and warbled about how 'we Londoners' feel about coming home, but he was only a few years out of Perth at the time he said it!

In such a milieu, to be Scottish was not at all desirable. Viewed from the Home Counties, the Scots were an unruly bunch who might build great ships, but had, within the memory of the parents of people then living, made armed rebellion against the crown and sent an invading army as far as Rugby. (That it was the best-behaved invasion force in the history of warfare was conveniently forgotten.) The Scots spoke a tongue which was barely comprehensible, had a different system of law and education, and the lower orders were often on terms of unseemly familiarity with their betters. Their national poet came from the former class and had harnessed literature to the cause of egalitarian values.

This opinion was ameliorated by the Romantic view of Scotland. The unruly clans could be seen as noble savages, the remote Highlands as suitable settings for paintings by Mr Landseer. That the Scots had been more than civil to George IV when he visited in 1820, and had shown him a good time (faking some very good 'traditions' for the purpose) was not necessarily a point in their favour, for George was a pretty disgraceful fellow and not the sort of person that the Britain of the later 19th century cared to remember. The queen had scotched such memories, however, by taking her recreation among the wild Highlanders, with the result that a certain kind of Scottishness had become acceptable.

The dichotomy between the two views of Scotland began a divide which has gripped Scotland ever since. On the one hand there is the real Scotland, which, like all complex entities, is difficult to approach; brilliance, virtue and vileness cohabiting with a lot of decent mediocrity; a people making their way in difficult circumstances. On the other there is a sanitised creation which looked a lot brighter and from which inconvenient reality can be omitted. This is the Scotland of the Landseer paintings, the picture postcards, the mawkish songs, the regimental colours and the tourist advertisements. It is a Scotland which is very useful to those who rule us and those who would sell us.

The second half of the 19th century was notable for the construction of a remarkable system of beliefs, of which a principal effect was to support the British state and to give authority to its functionaries. The monarchy was given status and respect where previously it had been held in contempt and ridicule; as the pinnacle of a great Empire it required to be beyond reproach. (Edward didn't help, but by the time he became active, the system was capable of accommodating his little foibles.) Rituals were invented, coronations and jubilees became great state occasions where before they had been shambolic. Honours and peerages were awarded galore and a small court expanded into a huge aristocracy in which gradations of place were carefully observed. The rest of society followed where their betters led. Gone was the easy familiarity of the 18th century, at least in England. (Norman Roger in his excellent study of the 18th-century Royal Navy remarks that the conjunction of easy familiarity of address with social stratification in conditions of close physical proximity among classes was not to be found on land. It was, until well into the 19th century, but only in Scottish cities such as Edinburgh's old town.)

A vast apparatus of orthodoxy was erected, endorsed by a willing public, and established as the permanent condition of things. What to one generation was novelty, to the next was commonplace and to its successors, tradition. An aura of permanence was given to a few decades which had seen more real change than had happened in as many previous centuries. The impression of permanence was given by appealing wherever possible to the sanction of tradition. Tradition was different from custom: custom was what people actually did; tradition was what they were supposed to do.

Traditions were adapted where possible and where there was no suitable candidate for conversion, they were invented. Ersatz Scottishness was grist to the mill, many of the recently invented traditions being put to good use: the clan tartans, the gorgeous military uniforms, the idyllic and romantic myth of Scottish history. An identity was constructed from which the nation has suffered ever since. I say suffered, for it was a false identity which rarely connected with reality and, because it was not founded in truth, was corrupted with the greatest of ease. Where there is no authenticity and where reality is kept at a distance, there is no objective criterion of what is good or bad, true or false. Hence there was nothing to impede the corruption of what Hugh Trevor-Roper calls the Highland Tradition of Scotland, and into ever more meretricious forms.

This process had its nadir in the music-hall Scots and the picture-postcard images of the Scots in the early years of the 20th century. It is difficult now to recall what ghastly travesties these allied media produced. Lauder was probably the most famous Scotsman of his age. One looks at his photographs and wonders that such a grotesque parody could ever have been tolerated, let alone raised to the status of cultural exemplar. The songs are still sung, but to an ageing audience, and they find few resonances in the performances of Rab C. Nesbit. The latter may not be an attractive figure but the values he promulgates are those of spiritual independence. He may be a disgusting drunk, but he is his own man. There is a world of difference between him and the red-nosed, short-kilted Scot of the *fin de siècle* picture postcard.

Scotland has changed a lot in the last quarter of a century. Some things are undoubtedly worse, but there can be little doubt that few thinking Scots would now connive at having their national self-image traduced as it was a hundred years ago, and that is a matter for rejoicing. Kitsch is still with us, but its function is different. The advent of heritage has given it a new lease of life, but heritage is obviously bogus, is on a par with Disneyland and the telly, and nobody mistakes it for history. The use of tartanry as a badge of Scottishness has transcended tradition and is like a metaphor which through overuse has lost all original signification. It has acquired a meaning of its own. That meaning is familiar to those who sell and those who buy. It has no more – and no less – dignity than a cigarette packet, or the incomprehensible logo by which corporate bureaucracy seeks vainly to attain individuality.

The place of Scotch whisky in all this is not hard to see. It was possible to replace brandy with whisky because of an already existing system of totems and values into which whisky fitted very neatly because of the rigid nature of Victorian society and the enormously powerful predisposition in favour of orthodoxy of opinion. Whisky having been established as a drink for British gentlemen, it was not necessary to show that it was good stuff, so it was not a difficult matter to sell blends in place of malts. Chaps took their whisky as they had their brandy, with ice and soda. This is a mode which effectively obliterates all nose and subtlety of taste. That didn't matter, for what most drinkers in the rigid social straitjacket of British society cared about was doing the right thing. That was the road of social acceptance.

A few Scots objected and a few malt distillers sought legal redress, helped curiously by the weights and measures department of Islington Borough Council. But by then (1911) it was too late and the big distillers won the day for blended whisky. By the 1930s, malt whisky had all but disappeared. Neil Gunn's *Whisky and Scotland*, published in the 1930s, is a cry in the wilderness and a diatribe against the big distillers who, Gunn maintained, had robbed Scotland of her birthright. Gunn was a couple of generations too early, but the seeds he sowed did not fall on barren ground. He did for many of us what he did for David Daiches: he put a case so powerfully and with such conviction that it stayed in the mind and sooner or later acted as a spur to action. False and factitious traditions may beget more and more preposterous offspring, but laughter and a taste for authenticity are not easily suppressed, especially when allied to the best of liquor.

> There was three kings into the east,
> Three kings both great and high,
> And they were sworn a solemn oath
> John Barleycorn should die.

Fortunately for Scotland's drinkers,

> John Barleycorn got up again
> And sore surprised them all.

Indeed he was never quite dead. He was to be found in Edinburgh literary circles as well as in Highland glens; he was to be found among left-wing nationalists and, Trevor Royle tells me, in the messes of Highland regiments. Stewart's Bar in Drummond Street in Edinburgh has bottled Glenlivet for longer than anyone there can remember. Alas, since this was written Mr Stewart has died and the bar has been sold. Its name has changed and it now sells alcopops to people who wouldn't know Glenlivet from grappa. *Sic transit gloria mundi.*

The folk who made the whisky knew what was the best stuff; the astonishing thing is that many of the folk who owned distilleries did not. Such is the influence of self-interest allied to ideology. The latter is not confined, as many would have us believe, to defunct Eastern empires.

The seeds lay awaiting the right conditions for germination. There were several of these. One was the revival of Scottish self-confidence, which took place from the early 1970s on, whose origins one can date back at least as far as the folk revival of the 1950s, and which, among other things, has given rise to political nationalism. It marginalised Scottish kitsch, and a noticeable corollary was a greater willingness on the part of many English people to take Scottish claims to quality seriously. (The great majority of Scotch Malt Whisky Society members are English.)

Another condition occured some time in the 1970s, when British gastronomy began to climb out of the pit into which it had fallen about a hundred years before. (This is an extraordinary phenomenon, which Derek Cooper has kindly agreed to write about.) We were not always satisfied with the gustatory standards of the 1950s.

A third has always been with us, though most have accepted what their masters told them, a sizeable minority of Scots have clung to a thrawn independence of judgement. It is common now as it was before, even in an era of relentless media manipulation.

As far as the drink goes, the wheel has come full circle with the Scotch Malt Whisky Society. At the time of writing, our list of whiskies is without peer. It was this that gave rise to the idea of a book about Scotland and whisky, to be written by some of our friends and leading Scots thinkers on the subject, some looking at what has happened and some looking at where we are today, but all telling the truth, without fear or favour, which is more than you can say for a lot of books about whisky. Their views are their own, and I do not see my editorial duties as including censorship.

Edinburgh
1 September 1991

Scots on Scotch

When Neil Gunn wrote (in 1935) that 'Before we know what whisky has meant to Scotland, presumably we must first have some idea of what Scotland means to herself'[1] he was edging towards an interesting notion. It is that Scotland and Scotch whisky have become, somehow, synonymous. There is certainly some truth in the idea. Whisky-making is one of those aspects of Scotland – like the landscape, the poet Burns, and the Scottish football team – which are invested with a transferred nationalism. This may not be healthy, but it is a fact. Scots are inordinately proud of their 'national' drink. Which begs the question: what kind of nation needs a national drink?

But the reasons for the phenomenon are not so hard to find. Scotland as an idea hardly exists outside the UK and the Scottish diaspora. Almost all foreigners regard Britain as England and England as Britain. The English do nothing to disabuse them of that misconception. Scotch whisky is one of the few players Scotland has left on the world stage. To many a truck driver in Boise, Idaho, or currency dealer in Singapore, the only trace of Scotland they might ever come across are the words 'Distilled and bottled in Scotland' on the label of a whisky bottle.

Which is why there is a special pain when distilleries close down or whisky companies are taken over. The angst voiced in Scotland over the Guinness takeover of the Distillers Company Ltd in 1986 startled the rest of Britain. English commentators, reasonable and liberal men for the most part, were at a loss to understand the grief. What was to them just another ailing (if important) British company was to many Scots an important part of Scotland itself.

And whisky and nationalism can be a fiery blend, as the Guinness boss Ernest Saunders found to his cost. When Saunders began his corporate raiding in Scotland in 1985 he was subjected, according to his son James, '. . . to the full blast of mistrust and resentment which appears to lurk north of the border when outsiders dare to intrude'.[2] In James Saunders' view it was the 'Scottish Mafia', led by Sir Norman Macfarlane, that brought his father down. At the same time national sentiment did nothing to stop the Scottish shareholders and institutions from selling their Distillers Company shares to the cross-border raiders. Profit, not patriotism, was the guiding star.

Of course, there is more to Scotland's love affair with whisky than just sentiment. Far more. The Scotch whisky industry is one of the most important components of the Scottish economy. Although it employs a modest 16,000 or so people directly (and many of those in England), many thousands more Scots are involved indirectly:

growing barley, making bottles, driving lorries and printing labels and whisky cartons (not to mention selling it in shops and pubs).

According to the Scotch Whisky Association, at the last count around £1.7 billion worth of Scotch was exported to 180 countries, accounting for around 20 per cent of Scotland's manufacturing exports (and 1.8 per cent of the British total). Volumes are calculated in litres of pure alcohol (LPA) and in 1990 almost 437 million LPA were exported. Whisky sold on the UK market is worth around £1 billion to Her Majesty's Government in VAT and excise duty.

The biggest single foreign market for Scotch remains the USA followed by France, but in recent years the Italians, Spaniards and Portuguese have been taking to Scotch in a big way. And although competition in Asia from the Japanese whisky-makers is fierce, Scotch is doing nicely in countries like Malaysia and Thailand. The world's thirst for good Scotch remains unslaked. The fear that 'white' spirit like gin, vodka and rum would clean up seems to have subsided. Scotch remains the world's tipple.

No one is quite sure whether it was the Scots who taught the Irish to make whisky or vice versa. It is possible that both Scots and Irish were taught the art by the Welsh (Britons). But whichever part of the Celtic nation came up with the idea, the Scots and Irish branches have been making '*uisge beatha*' (Gaelic for the water of life) since early mediaeval times. For centuries whisky distilling seems to have been confined to the Gaelic-speaking uplands of Scotland. The first official mention of whisky in Lowland Scotland is in the exchequer rolls of 1494 which notes 'eight bolls of malt to Friar John Cor wherewith to make aquavitae'.

Nor did the hazards of whisky quaffing go unnoticed. An act of the Scots Parliament of 1579 prohibited whisky distilling (at least by the lower orders). This was not so much out of fear of drunkenness, but concern for the grain stocks needed to feed the population. This prohibition was almost certainly ignored. In the late 16th century the King of Scots was in no position to enforce his laws in every Highland glen. The Gaelic folk art of whisky-making went on regardless of Edinburgh's strictures.

Surprisingly perhaps, it took the Scottish authorities another 150 or so years to realise the money-spinning potential of whisky. It was not until 1644 that the Scots Parliament slapped an excise tax on whisky which lapsed at the restoration of Charles II in 1660 and was then reimposed in 1693. An exception was made for Duncan Forbes of Culloden, that great supporter of the Orange ascendancy, who was given the right to distil and sell duty-free whisky from barley grown on his estate at Ferintosh in Easter Ross. (The Forbes family managed to hold on to this profitable privilege until 1785.)

In 1707 the fledgling British Parliament established a Board of Excise which, six years later, slapped an English-style malt tax on the makers of Scotch whisky. Although the new tax was set at half the English level it was bitterly resented. There were bloody riots in Edinburgh and Glasgow. And, naturally, there was a proliferation of illegal stills all over the Highlands. For most of the 18th century the British government's 'excisemen' (one of whom was Robert Burns) waged an unsuccessful war against the upland whisky makers and salesmen.

Although the whisky smugglers have become folk heroes in Scotland, they were no joke. There were many serious gangsters amongst them. Some were hard-bitten Jacobites who'd fought at Falkirk and Culloden and knew how to wield a stabbing dirk or heavy cudgel, which they never hesitated to use on the excisemen. They were efficient, cunning, well organised and had a lot of public support in the Lowland towns where they peddled their whisky. Their descendants were still working the illicit stills well into the 1960s.

The Reverend Thomas Guthrie, one of the founders of the Free Church of Scotland, has left a vivid description of 30 mounted smugglers trooping through his home town of Brechin in Angus. The outlaws had sold their wares and were making their way home. As they rode through Brechin they beat time with their cudgels on the empty casks slung over their shaggy horses. It was done, according to Guthrie, to 'the great amusement of the public and mortification of the excisemen who had nothing for it but to bite their nails and stand, as best they could, the raillery of the smugglers and the laughter of the people'.[3]

Whisky taxing proved to be one of the many points of contention between Scottish and English interests. In the 18th century a thriving gin-distilling industry had grown up in parts of England – notably London, Liverpool and Bristol – and the English distillers did their best to keep Scotch out of their markets. They were particularly aggrieved by the fact that they were taxed more heavily than their Scots counterparts, and lobbied the British government to do something about it.

The government obliged by slapping an extra 'export duty' of sixpence for every gallon sent out of Scotland. Which was enough to bankrupt a large handful of legal distillers and prove once again that crime – in the shape of illicit distilling – did pay. In a desperate attempt to stamp out the illicit whisky makers of the Gaedhealtachdt the British government passed an act in 1814 which banned – north of the Highland line – any still with a capacity less than 500 gallons. Big was beautiful in the government's eyes. Or, at least, big was visible.

Not that all the *sub rosa* whisky making was confined to the glens and straths of the Highlands. The Scottish lowlanders were becoming deft whisky makers too. In 1777 the excise calculated that there were eight legal stills in Edinburgh and around 400 illicit operations. Illegal distilleries flourished in the more remote corners of the border hills, the Campsies and the southern fringes of the Grampians.

Whisky drinking was given something of a boost in 1822 during the ludicrous royal visit to Scotland of King George IV. The portly Hanoverian had hardly anchored in Scottish waters before he was calling for a measure of Glenlivet whisky (which was an illicit brew). The fat king's enthusiasm for whisky appears to have been genuine. On a trip to Dublin he spent the journey sinking copious amounts of Irish whiskey, '. . . singing many joyous songs'.

(Ever since then, the whisky makers have relished their royal associations. Brand names are full of royalisms: 'Queen Anne', 'Highland Queen', 'Spey Royal', 'Prince Charlie', 'Chivas Regal', 'Royal Stewart', 'Queen's Own', 'King's Ransom', 'Prince Consort' and many more. Even more use is made of the 'Royal warrants' which three of the Royal households – the Queen's, the Queen Mother's and the Prince of Wales' – award to deserving companies.)

When the fearsome disease *phylloxera vastatrix* devastated the French vineyards in the 1870s and 1880s it rendered Cognac brandy both scarce and very, very expensive. At a stroke, the favourite tipple of the British gentry and aristocracy was snatched away. Something had to take its place.

The condition of the British drinks market, post-*phylloxera*, was elegantly summed up in 1887 by Alfred Barnard. He wrote:

> French Brandy is, as an article of general consumption, hopelessly discredited . . . Rum, for some occult reason, nobody that is anybody drinks, except for the medicinal treatment of a cold. Gin, with all its many merits, fails to gain new drinkers, while the old consumers seem to be dying out. The opportunity for Whisky is, therefore, overwhelming. What will it do with it?

As Barnard saw it, the race was on between the makers of Scotch whisky and Irish whiskey.

> England is the market in which both Irish and Scotch Distillers are contending for the pre-eminence; while Caledonia drinks her own Whisky, Hibernia prefers *her* own make, so that the Saxon taste is the pivot upon which, in these days, hangs the prosperity of the Distilling Trade of either nation.[4]

In fact, the Scots won the race for the 'Saxon taste' quite comfortably. In 1880 the Scots and Irish distillers were lying roughly neck and neck. The Scots were selling 1.8 million proof gallons in England compared to the Irish total of 1.6 million. But 20 years later the Scots were doing 7.1 million compared to the Irish distillers' 4.2 million. There is some irony in the fact that the Scots relied heavily on the technology put in place by the Irishman Aeneas Coffey.

How the Scotch distillers won such a slice of the English market is a story in itself. They hit Britain with an ingenious marketing campaign that gradually transformed Scotch into a national and then a world drink. The press was blitzed with advertisements depicting toffs and their ladies sinking glasses of Scotch (or Scotch and soda). Dewar's erected on the South Bank of the Thames a huge electric Highlander whose kilt seemed to sway as he sipped on his glass of whisky. The brilliant comic artist Tom Browne was hired to create the monocled gent 'Johnnie Walker' ('born 1820 and still going strong'). It was one of the most sustained, ingenious and effective sales drives in the history of British commerce.

And it helped that the industry was in the hands of some remarkably able men. The late 19th and early 20th centuries were the days of the great whisky 'barons': John and Tommy Dewar, Alexander Walker, James Buchanan, Peter Mackie, James Stevenson and William Ross. Between them they ran the 'Big Five' firms that dominated the market: John Dewar, John Walker, White Horse, James Buchanan and the Distillers Company Ltd (DCL).

As the market for Scotch expanded the industry's urge to 'rationalise' grew. The driving force behind this process was the most impressive of the whisky barons, William Ross, the secretary and general manager of DCL (itself the product of a six-firm merger in 1877). Ross was a firm believer that big was beautiful and that if Scotch wanted to conquer the world it would need at least one giant to crash through the commercial and bureaucratic jungles. Ross's dream was to get all 'Big Five' Scotch whisky makers into one corporate harness.

But rounding them all up took decades. It was 1925 before Ross managed to coax John Dewar and James Buchanan to join with DCL, and 1927 before White Horse was in the trace. Nor was that the end of DCL's acquisitions. In 1927 DCL bought Bulloch Lade. A decade later, in 1937, they took on board William Sanderson & Son, makers of the famous VAT 69.

But no sooner had Scotch begun to establish itself on the world market than it was dealt a crippling blow in the form of American Prohibition. The Volstead Act, passed by Congress in 1919 and activated in 1920, was the result of generations of pressure by the powerful temperance lobby in the USA. Campaigners like the Anti-Saloon League argued that booze was subverting the morals and morale of the American people. The Devil Drink had to be driven out. From sea to shining sea. And if that spelled ruin for the liquor producers of Europe and Canada, too bad.

Officially, there was nothing the Scotch Distillers could do about it. Unofficially, it was another matter. The Scotch whisky makers were not about to abandon the biggest and most promising market on earth. They knew the demand for whisky was there. They calculated that Prohibition would not last. They were determined to keep the American public's taste for good Scotch whisky alive. So they instigated a little-known but highly successful war against Uncle Sam.

Scotland's *sub rosa* campaign against the United States prohibition agencies is one of the untold tales of the 20th century. The liquor war was not – as Hollywood seems to believe – fought exclusively between federal agents and Italian-American 'bootleggers'. Just as important (and almost as deadly) were the battles waged at sea between the US Navy and Coastguard and the mainly British liquor pirates, dubbed 'rum runners' by the American public. Many of those smugglers were funded by the 'syndicates' of City of London businessmen, who in turn were supplied by the respectable Scotch distillers.

The liquor war lasted almost 13 years, from 1920 to 1933, when Prohibition was finally scrapped. Dozens of ships were sunk, impounded, looted and damaged. Fortunes were made and lost. And despite a Liquor Treaty of 1924 between the British and American governments, the activities of the Scotch whisky industry and its disreputable offspring strained British and American diplomatic relations badly. The Americans suspected – with some justification – that His Majesty's Government was turning a blind eye to the activities of the booze runners.

The system that the Scotch whisky barons put in place was complex in detail but simple in essence. What happened was this: the distillers and blenders set up a string of 'agents' in Canada, Cuba, Bermuda, the British Honduras, the Bahamas and the tiny French colonies of St Pierre and Miquelon off the coast of Nova Scotia. These agents then imported – quite legally – huge amounts of Scotch into their respective territories. Whisky imports to the Bahamas, for example, soared from 944 gallons of Scotch in 1918 to more than 386,000 gallons in 1922, two years into Prohibition. The French islands of St Pierre and Miquelon had a tiny population of less than 6,000 people. But they imported more than 116,000 gallons of Scotch in 1922 – which works out at 20 gallons of whisky for every man, woman and child on the islands. Other stocks of whisky (and rum, brandy and wine) were held in Belize City, the Cayman Islands, Cuba and the Dutch Antilles.

All these places were, of course, nothing more than staging posts or *entrepots* for huge quantities of Scotch. From these offshore dumps the whisky was loaded into a variety of sailing schooners and tramp steamers and shipped into international waters off the coast of New York and New Jersey. There they lay at anchor until their cargo of Scotch was bought by 'bootleggers' operating speedboats and fast launches (known as 'contact boats') and occasionally small sea-planes.

The waters off the New York/New Jersey coast became known as 'Rum Row' and the ships that lay there were nothing more than floating wholesale warehouses stuffed with booze. Sometimes more than 100 liquor ships would lie in the 150-mile arc between Long Island and Atlantic

City. And as the liquor armada was lying in international waters (i.e. outside the 12-mile limit) there was little that the US government could do about it, except try to intercept the fast launches of the New York and New Jersey gangsters.

Not all the liquor sold on Rum Row came via the Bahamas or St Pierre. Many cargoes were shipped directly out of Scotland (usually from the Clyde). A young Scot called Alastair Moray described an eight-month voyage in an elderly flat-bottomed schooner called *The Cask* which left the Clyde at the end of 1923 carrying 20,000 cases of 'Black and White', 'Old Claymore' and 'White Horse'. The eight-man crew of Scots, Finns and Swedes were kitted out with Webley revolvers and a heavy machine-gun to protect themselves against the 'go through guys', freelance gangsters who preyed on rum runners and bootleggers alike.

It was an elaborate but remarkably effective system. It ensured that millions of gallons of Scotch found its way into the illegal bars, speakeasies and clubs of New York, New Jersey, Philadelphia and Boston. Most of it was heavily diluted (or 'cut') by the gangsters so that one bottle of Scotch in a speakeasy was worth four or five times its value in a cargo hold. For that reason they preferred dark and heavy whiskies which could be cut without too much loss of taste. Some pundits claim that the diluting habits of the bootleggers saved many an American liver and gave the American public a taste for 'light' whisky which it has never lost.

None of this would have been possible without the connivance of the British colonies in and around the Caribbean. The Bahamas in particular boomed during the Prohibition years. Whisky was stored in the government's own bonded warehouses at six dollars a case, and cash-flush crews from the booze ships kept the Nassau flophouses, pubs and whorehouses in business. One official history of the Bahamas traces the prosperity of the islands back to 'the Prohibition era when the islands were an ideal base for alcohol smugglers'.

This blatant whisky running could not be ignored. The American government (rightly) saw it as a direct challenge to the laws and sovereignty of the United States and were determined to stamp it out. They leaned heavily on the British government (and its colonial offspring) and forced them to sign the Liquor Treaty of 1924. The British government promised to do its best, but claimed that its hands were tied by International Maritime Law. The Americans fumed while the whisky flowed in.

The war at sea probably reached its peak in 1925 when Rear Admiral Frederick C. Billard put together a fleet of more than 400 US Navy and Coastguard vessels, plus squadrons of aircraft, in a vain attempt to stop the booze runners. British ships were boarded, seized, forced into American ports and impounded. One British skipper accused of whisky running committed suicide. The British schooner *Eastwood* (a notorious whisky runner) was chased more than 30 miles out into the open sea by the Coastguard cutter *Seneca* and shot to pieces by heavy machine-guns. It was a miracle that no one was killed.

The British-owned ship *I'm Alone* was not so lucky. In March 1929 she was sailing 200 miles out in the Gulf of Mexico with a cargo of Scotch, rye, rum and champagne, when she was overhauled by the US cutter *Dexter* and ordered to heave to. The schooner's captain – a Boer War veteran called Jack Bardell – refused, and the American gunship opened fire. The British ship sank like a stone, killing the ship's bo'sun and leaving the rest of the eight-man crew (including a black cook from Belize called William Wordsworth) floundering in the Gulf of Mexico. The Americans hauled the men out of the water, clapped them in irons and transported them to New Orleans, where they were thrown into the Parish Gaol until the British, French and Canadian governments sorted out the mess. Irate diplomatic notes flew between governments. An international commission later awarded the owners of *I'm Alone* compensation and decided that the *Dexter* had been out of order to send the British ship to the bottom of the ocean.

Such incidents were, of course, signs of the frustration felt by the American authorities. American officers like Eugene Blake, captain of the *Seneca*, were plainly outraged by the way in which the US law was being flouted and determined to punish the perpetrators. And when things got too hot at sea, the whisky pirates switched to running their goods through the long and largely unguarded border with Canada. Imports of Scotch into Canada soared, and most of it found its way into the USA. Detroit became *the* booze gateway to the USA. Huge ingenuity was expended dodging the US customs men.

One of the most resourceful of the whisky smugglers was Samuel Bronfman, who acquired Joseph Seagram & Sons in 1928, and then a string of distilleries and blending houses in Scotland: Milton, Glen Keith, Keith Maltings, Keith Bonds and Chivas Brothers of Aberdeen. According to the gangster-prince, Charles 'Lucky' Luciano, Bronfman was 'bootleggin' enough whisky across the Canadian border to double the size of Lake Erie'.[5]

No matter what the American authorities did, the whisky always got through. No matter how many planes, ships and Coastguard cutters they threw into the line, the blockade never held. The bizarre alliance of Scotch distillers, gung-ho British seamen and the American underworld proved too much for the US Navy and US Coastguard. And while the respectable businessmen of Scotland and the City of London stayed in the shadows as much as they could, they were as ruthless in their own way as Lucky Luciano and Alphonse Capone. When Sir Alexander Walker of John Walker & Co. was asked by a Royal Commission in 1931 whether the whisky producers of Scotland would ever stop running liquor into the USA, he hardly hesitated. 'Certainly not!' he told the commissioners.

When Prohibition ended in 1933, the Scotch whisky industry resumed its campaign to become one of the world's great drinks. The Second World War was a setback, of course. Whisky distilling almost ground to a complete halt. But there is a (fairly plausible) theory that it boosted Scotch in the long term. The Second World War allowed the armies of Poles, Dutch, Norwegians, Czechs, French and Americans who drifted through wartime Britain, the chance to acquire the taste for Scotch. They took that taste back to their own countries. And at a time when a bottle of Scotch was almost worth its weight in gold. Scotch acquired a cachet with that generation which it never lost.

The money-spinning potential of Scotch was not lost on Winston Churchill (who was a brandy drinker himself). In 1945 he instructed the Ministry of Food: 'On no account reduce the amount of barley for whisky. It takes two years to mature and is an invaluable export and dollar earner. Having regard to our difficulties about export, it would be improvident not to preserve the characteristic element of British ascendancy.'[6] Which is an interesting final flourish; the old Tory warhorse plainly saw Scotch as an instrument of British imperialism (social as well as commercial).

Just why Scotch whisky did so well in the post-war boom is hard to understand. The industry's marketing was good, but not that good. The drink just seems to have captured the palate of the industrialised world. The giant DCL did particularly well. The Japanese, for example, found 'White Horse' greatly to their taste. All over Europe and Africa, Johnnie Walker was the top person's drink. Americans and Canadians could see nothing finer than a bottle of Dewar's. There is a legend that wealthy Nigerians began squirrelling stock of Johnnie Walker in the way that other people hoard gold, as a hedge against inflation.

For whatever reason, Scotch boomed worldwide. The proof is in the export figures. In 1946 exports of Scotch whisky amounted to 5.9 million proof gallons. Ten years later, in 1956, the figure was 16.4 million proof gallons. In 1966 that figure had more than doubled to 41.5 million proof gallons. A decade on it had doubled again to 91.8 million proof gallons. Two years later, in 1978, it had reached a whopping 105.6 proof gallons, or more than *20 times* the export level of 1946. It was an astonishing growth record, which produced euphoric shareholders and a complacent industry.

But there was a price to be paid. The success of the Scotch distillers attracted some big corporate predators. In the 1960s and 1970s no fewer than 77 distilleries changed hands, and most of them were sold to companies outside of Scotland. And although the British government paid lip service to a 'regional' policy, only *one* takeover was ever referred to the Monopolies and Mergers Commission (MMC), the agency which decided whether takeovers were in the public interest.

The referral was in 1980 when the Canadian giant Hiram Walker tried to buy up Highland Distilleries, makers of the enormously successful 'Famous Grouse' brand. The MMC knocked back the Canadian bid without too much hesitation. One reason the MMC gave was that the takeover would be bad for Scotland in that it would 'have an adverse effect on career opportunities in

Scotland since Highland's top management will be deprived of the opportunity to take strategic decisions'.[7]

Such British government concern for the wider Scottish interest was never repeated. In 1984 the then Secretary of State for Trade and Industry, Norman Tebbit, issued a new set of guidelines for takeovers and mergers. The so-called 'regional interest' was no longer to count for anything. The 'Tebbit Rules' (as they were quickly dubbed) left the Scotch whisky industry wide open to takeover.

Not that there was much takeover activity in the early 1980s. The industry suffered grievously in the economic blizzard that swept across Britain and, to a lesser extent, the rest of the industrialised world. Many fine distilleries perished in the cold winds. Worst hit was the giant DCL. In 1983 DCL announced plans to close down no fewer than 11 of their distilleries: Benronach, Brora, Dallas Dhu, Glenalbyn, Glen Mhor, Glenlochy, North Port, Knockdhu, Port Ellen, Saint Magdalene and Carsebridge.

Parts of rural Scotland reeled under the unexpected blow. The bad days of the 1930s were back. Alan Gray, of the highly regarded firm of Glasgow stockbrokers Campbell Neill, did not help by ruminating that 'All drinks have their time and Scotch has had a pretty good run. But there now has got to be better marketing to win back younger people who have gone over to other drinks.'

Other drinks! Gray had identified (or at least publicly articulated) the problem which had been bothering the industry for some time: Scotch was no longer fashionable. The new generation of drinkers was dropping Scotch in favour of 'light' spirits like white rum, gin and vodka. Stylish young people preferred a colourless liquor they could mix into a variety of concoctions. Strange-looking cocktails, with even stranger-sounding names, were replacing 'Scotch on the rocks' as the drink of the North American and European *cognoscenti*.

The signs were ominous. The decline seemed inexorable. In 1984 and 1985 DCL announced another round of cuts. The VAT 69 plant at South Queensferry and the White Horse plant in Glasgow were shut down with the loss of more than 700 jobs. A few months later, another dozen or so small distilleries were mothballed, and another 180 jobs vanished in areas that could ill afford to lose them. Scotland's biggest whisky maker – with 36 per cent of the industry's output and 127 brands on the shelves – was plainly in serious trouble.

Not that success guaranteed independence. Highland Distilleries found in 1980 that success attracts predators, and Arthur Bell & Sons of Perth were to find the same, to their cost. One of the most successful whisky makers in Scotland, Arthur Bell & Sons had boomed. Under their hard-charging chief executive Raymond Miquel (the son of a French chef), Bell's whisky had become the fastest-selling brand in Britain. By early 1980 it had around 35 per cent of the home market. Miquel's success was reflected in the company's pre-tax profits: £4.1 million in 1975; £31.4 million in 1983. By 1985 Miquel had transformed Arthur Bell & Sons into one of the tastiest corporate morsels in Scotland.

Miquel was to be given a rude awakening – quite literally. On 14 June 1985 he was telephoned in his hotel room in Chicago in the middle of the night to be told that the London-based but Irish-owned Guinness group had made a £330 million takeover bid for Arthur Bell & Sons. At which point the fate of Arthur Bell & Sons became a (Scottish) national issue. Raymond Miquel and his supporters immediately began erecting the 'Scottish ring fence' which had saved the Royal Bank of Scotland from the raiders from Hong Kong. Arthur Bell & Sons came to represent the best of Scotland. Whisky and Scotland became synonymous.

But the Guinness boss, Ernest Saunders, had been well briefed on Scottish sensibilities. He immediately began courting the Scottish press. He hired Scottish public relations men. He was always available to Scottish journalists in search of a 'steer' and a quote. He even exercised his considerable charm on the staff of the tiny *Perthshire Advertiser* (who were Miquel supporters to a man). Saunders' public exhortations were always laced with references to the Scottish interest: 'We will make Bell's a successful company once again, successful for Scottish jobs and for Scottish exports . . .'

It worked. The Scottish ring fence swayed, cracked and then collapsed. Guinness upped their offer to more than £340 million, and institutional and private shareholders fell over themselves to accept. And when Peter Tyrie, one of Miquel's directors, broke ranks, closely followed by the Perth-based insurance firm General Accident, it was over. Ernest Saunders and Guinness had won. The Scottish ring fence was down. The most successful distiller in Scotland had slipped out of Scottish ownership. Politicians and commentators of various stripes squirmed, but there was nothing they could do.

The cloud hanging over the Scotch whisky industry darkened in February 1986 when it was announced that the Tomatin Distillery near Inverness – the biggest malt distillery in Scotland – had been taken over by a Japanese consortium. And to add insult to injury, the companies involved were Okura, a middling-sized trading company, and Takara Shuzo, who made highly coloured, highly flavoured soft drinks for the Japanese market.

But the Bell's and Tomatin takeovers were pinpricks to Scottish pride compared to the next blow. The next company to slip out of Scottish control was the biggest of them all – Distillers Company Ltd (DCL). Although outwardly prosperous, the whisky giant had a number of serious problems. The Thalidomide tragedy of the 1960s had been a public relations disaster which still lingered. An EEC price equalisation ruling stopped DCL selling Johnnie Walker for more money abroad than at home. The result was that the brand was withdrawn from the UK market, which left a gap into which Bell's and The Famous Grouse galloped. Although profitable, DCL was about half as profitable as it should have been. And it was sitting on an enormous pile of assets – offices, warehouses, factories, distilleries, land – all over the world.

The flagship of the Scottish whisky industry was, in fact, a prime target for takeover. The first shots in the takeover were fired by James Gulliver, the Scots-born boss of the Argyll Group (a drinks and grocery chain). Gulliver spent a large sum of money buying DCL shares, dithered, then finally made a bid – £1.87 billion – at the beginning of December 1985. Gulliver played the Scottish card. He made his announcement at a press conference in Edinburgh and promised, hand on heart, that if he won control of DCL then the company's headquarters would be shifted from London to Edinburgh. The flagship would be repatriated, so to speak.

Then, just as it seemed that Gulliver's bid for DCL would go ahead, Ernest Saunders and Guinness entered the fray. On 20 January 1986, Saunders announced to the world that Guinness planned to 'merge' with DCL, and that Guinness was prepared to pay £2.2 billion for the privilege – i.e. £400 million more than Gulliver. The bid worked out at a whopping £6.04 per share. It seemed a handsome offer for an ailing company.

And Saunders played *his* Scottish card even more strongly than Gulliver. Sir Thomas Risk, a governor of the Bank of Scotland, was to be chairman. The respected Edinburgh lawyer Charles Fraser was to be a director. The new Guinness/DCL conglomerate was to be run from Scotland instead of London. There would be high-grade jobs aplenty in Edinburgh. Saunders and his wife Carole spent the next few months very publicly looking for a suitable house in Edinburgh's New Town.

Before the deal could go through, Saunders had to persuade the Office of Fair Trading (OFT) that a Guinness/DCL merger would not be against the public interest. Others tried to argue that it was against *Scotland's* interest to allow such an important company to slip out of Scottish control. In March 1986, the OFT accepted the 'Tebbit Rules', decided that the Scottish interest counted for nothing and declined to refer the bid to the Monopolies and Mergers Commission.

The story of how Saunders and his colleagues went on to illegally manipulate the Guinness share price upwards to ensure its acceptability to DCL's shareholders is a saga in itself. Simply put, Saunders arranged for some of the most influential businessmen in Britain – Sir Jack Lyons, Gerald Ronson, Anthony Parnes, Roger Seelig and others – to buy Guinness shares to keep the price high. They were then paid a 'success fee' for their troubles. Such share-buying 'concert parties' are totally illegal, and Saunders and his fellow conspirators ended up in gaol.

But not before the wheeling and dealing had worked. On Friday, 18 April, Saunders announced that Guinness had obtained more than 50 per cent of the DCL shares. DCL was now a subsidiary of Guinness and Ernest Saunders was at the head of a company valued at £3.7 billion. The flagship of the Scotch whisky industry had been boarded and taken over. Scotland's biggest industrial company was no longer Scottish. The lavish party to celebrate the 'merger' of Guinness with DCL was held, quite suitably, in Buckinghamshire.

And once DCL had been trussed up, all the promises to

Scotland were abandoned. Sir Thomas Risk was eased out as company chairman. Risk and Charles Fraser were painted by Saunders as pettyfogging 'Little Scotlanders'. And the plans to move the Guinness/Distillers HQ to Edinburgh were dropped as 'impractical'. The fact that this move to Scotland had been promised in the official offer document was ignored. The ensuing barrage of protests from Scottish politicians, businessmen and civic leaders was shrugged off as so much misguided nationalism.

The Guinness/DCL affair threw into relief some marked differences between Scottish and English perceptions. The Scots believed they had been promised the moon then sold down the river. Even Tory MPs like Nicholas Fairbairn and Bill Walker were aggrieved. In fact, Fairbairn was one of four MPs who tabled an early day motion deploring Saunders for 'wilfully misleading Ministers and Members of Parliament, by making promises to move the headquarters of the Guinness Distillers group to Scotland . . . while clearly having no intention of doing any such thing . . .'

Most English commentators, on the other hand, thought Saunders was right to put the health of the companies before any 'regional' (i.e. Scottish) considerations. A typically staunch Saunders supporter was *The Times* financial writer Kenneth Fleet. 'The Clans in Glasgow and Charlotte Square are baying for blood,' Fleet assured readers, 'and the Scottish media bathe daily in mass hysteria. The blood in particular they want is Ernest Saunders', who has been subject to malign and racist insults of a despicable kind.'

Although the 'Scottish Mafia', as they were called by the London press, did eventually succeed in ousting Saunders from Guinness Distillers, the damage had been done. The giant of the Scotch whisky industry was lost to

Scottish control. The company created by William Ross, the wiliest of the Scotch whisky magnates, had slipped away from Scotland.

The DCL takeover was a stunning blow to the self-respect of industrial Scotland. Distilling was, after all, the archetypal Scottish industry. If the powerful Scotch whisky industry was not safe from corporate marauders, who was? The loss of DCL seemed to many Scots commentators to reflect the parlous and politically defenceless state of Scotland itself.

The issues raised by the DCL takeover were certainly troubling. And one of them was the question, just how Scots is Scotch? The answer, so far as ownership is concerned, is not very. An assiduous piece of research by Jim Love of Strathclyde University reveals that a mere 25 per cent of the Scotch whisky industry remains in Scottish hands. In 1989, when Love did his research, English companies (like Guinness and Allied Lyons) owned the lion's share of 57.3 per cent; Canadians and Americans had a 9.4 per cent share; the Europeans owned 6.2 per cent; and the Japanese had taken a 2.1 per cent slice.[8] Since this was written, things have got a little better. Highland has resisted the blandishments of the Japanese and Kindall has bought the Whyte & Mackay brand, previously owned by Jim Beam Brands, back into Scottish ownership.

The iron fact is that the whisky business, Scotland's pride and sometime joy, is overwhelmingly a foreign-owned industry. The fate of the great brand names like Dewar's White Label, Dimple Haig, VAT 69, Queen Anne and Johnnie Walker, and all the rest, will be decided by people whose interests lie outside Scotland. The distilleries, blending houses and bottling plants of Scotland are bought and sold on the world market like any other commodity. Scotch whisky is now as much a part of the 'branch factory economy' as the offshore oil industry or the electronics firms of 'Silicon Glen'.

Which is a situation not without its poignancy. One of the most famous malt whisky distilleries in Scotland used to be the Ben Nevis Distillery at Fort William. Founded in 1825 by one John Macdonald, the distillery's most famous product was a whisky called 'Long John', named after the founder's lanky father. The family were Keppoch Macdonalds, notorious Jacobites.

On his visit to the Ben Nevis Distillery the amiable Alfred Barnard waxed lyrical about the surrounding fir plantations which were 'in striking contrast to the background of the mountain [Ben Nevis] whose projections intrude themselves up to the very walls of the Distillery'. Ben Nevis was the Highland distillery *par excellence*.

But in 1989 the Ben Nevis Distillery was bought by the Japanese firm Nikka Whisky Distilling. The malt whisky distilled in the shadow of Ben Nevis is now shipped by Nikka back to Japan to be blended with Japanese whisky to slake the thirst of the growing Asian market. As Japanese whisky is now Scotch whisky's biggest and most fearsome competitor, many Scots inside and outside the whisky business regard this kind of sell-out – like the export of malt whisky in bulk tankers – as a form of industrial and commercial *hara-kiri*.

The predicament of the Scotch whisky industry is an interesting metaphor for the helpless state of Scotland itself. To that extent, Neil Gunn was right. Nothing could be more Scottish than Scotch whisky. But what happens to it in the next few decades will not be decided in Scotland. It was take more than the alchemy of the distillers to alter that fact.

REFERENCES

[1] Gunn, Neil, *Whisky and Scotland*, 1935.

[2] Saunders, James, *Nightmare: Ernest Saunders and the Guinness Affair*, 1988.

[3] Daiches, David, *Scotch Whisky: Its Past and Present*, 1969.

[4] Barnard, Alfred, *The Whisky Distilleries of the United Kingdom*, 1877.

[5] Gosch, Martin & Hammer, Richard, *The Luciano Testament*, 1975.

[6] McDowall, R.J.S., *The Whiskies of Scotland*, 1967.

[7] HMSO, 'Hiram Walker Gooderham & Worts Ltd and the Highland Distilleries Company Ltd: a report on the proposed merger, HC 743', 1980.

[8] Love, J.H., *The Changing Structure of the Scotch Whisky Industry*, 1989.

The figure of the kilted Highland soldier is one of the world's most potent advertising symbols: to people everywhere he sums up a sense of Scotland in a way that few other images can, and if he did not exist, the Scottish Tourist Board would have been hard pushed to invent him. In his kilt and sporran, his feathered bonnet and white spats he is a colourful yet utterly respectable figure; marching in serried ranks behind the pipes and drums against the dramatic backcloth of Edinburgh or Stirling Castle, he is as familiarly Caledonian as the bonnie banks of Loch Lomond or the heather-covered road to the Isles. Place him on a tin of shortbread, a tourist brochure or, even better, a bottle of whisky, and he becomes an instantly marketable commodity.

And why not? From the very earliest times Scots have

made good soldiers, indeed, it has been observed that war is an essential ingredient in the Scots psychological make-up. The nation's history is bloody with battles, some fought against the nearest neighbour, England; many more fought amongst the Scots themselves, family against family, clan against clan. As with many other countries in Europe's peripheries – Albania, Prussia, Switzerland, for example – war became something of a homespun industry and, like whisky, one that could be exported. From the 16th century onwards, Scots mercenaries fought in the service of France, Spain, Russia and Sweden, playing fast and loose with the destinies of the monarchs who paid their wages.

They were widely recognised as a warrior race and the Scottish soldier was renowned as a tough and uncompromising swordsman who could march long distances on minimal rations and still be ready to go into battle. It has been estimated that during the Thirty Years War, 20,000 Scots served under King Gustavus Adolphus of Sweden while a further 10,000 opposed them in the allied armies of King Louis XIII of France. At various times during the same period there were 3,000 Scots in the Russian army, 6,000 in Holland and many more in the armies of Prussia and Spain. Amongst them was Sir John Hepburn, a Scots soldier of fortune who served Gustavus Adolphus before transferring his men and his loyalties to the King of France. In 1633 he raised the regiment known as the *Royal Ecossais*, which became the closest guard to the French throne. For his services, Hepburn became a Marshal of France and his regiment remained in French service until the restoration of King Charles III when it was recalled to Britain: as the Royal Scots it is the oldest line infantry regiment in the British Army and it is still numbered the 1st of Foot. (Under the 1991 army reforms it was amalgamated with the King's Own Scottish Borderers.)

Scots fighting prowess was not just confined to the fields of Flanders or to the north German plain. At home in Scotland, Borderers raided their English counterparts with grim enthusiasm and the wearing of arms was a familiar sight. Retainers in the service of the nobility and the landowners were obliged to settle their masters' quarrels or to follow them to war. This was especially true in the Highlands where clan chiefs supported successive Jacobite attempts to return the Roman Catholic Stewart dynasty to the throne of Britain. 'I'll share the fate of my Prince,' said Cameron of Lochiel when he pledged his support to Prince Charles Edward Stuart in 1745, adding, 'and so shall every man over whom nature or fortune hath given me power'. His message was clear: his clansmen were bound by family and tribal ties to join him in the last fateful Jacobite adventure.

Although the Highlanders of Bonnie Prince Charlie's army enjoyed initial success against inferior government opposition during the autumn of 1745, they met their match eight months later on the field of Culloden near Inverness. There, on 16 April 1746, they learned the grim lesson that clan loyalty and the aggression of the traditional Highland charge was no match for the tactics and the discipline of a modern army. The Duke of Cumberland, who led the government forces, had seasoned troops under his command, many of whom had served with him during earlier European campaigns. They were all volunteers, English, Irish and Scots – for amongst their number were the men of three Lowland battalions which would later become better known as regiments of the Scottish Division of the modern British Army. Named after their commanding officer at the time, these were St Clair's (The Royal Scots), Campbell's (The Royal Highland Fusiliers) and Sempill's (The King's Own Scottish Borderers).

In the immediate aftermath of the uprising the British government thought it best to disarm the clans and savagely pacify the Highlands. Many of the best military commanders and men of the Prince's army fled into exile or were killed, but the Highlanders' fighting qualities were too impressive to ignore. From 1756 onwards their martial ardour was channelled by William Pitt into the service of his imperial dreams. Highland regiments fought with General James Wolfe in Canada and then, later, in the American War of Independence, where the rough terrain of the Atlantic states suited their abilities as skirmishers, skilled in fieldcraft and irregular warfare. 'They are hardy, intrepid, accustomed to a rough country,' said Wolfe, 'and no great mischief if they fall.' In addition to praising that staunchness of character, Wolfe also learned another lesson: the value of the bagpipes in adding steel to the soul of the Scottish soldier. During the struggle for the Heights of Abraham in 1759, Wolfe forbade his Highlanders to play their pipes during the night attack. The men were repulsed, forcing the General to rescind his order. 'Then let them blow as they like,' he said. 'And send them on again.' The Highlanders took their objective.

By the beginning of the 19th century Scotland was recognised as a valuable recruiting ground, especially the Highlands, which supplied ten distinct regiments, five of which were designated 'Highland' in the army lists – 42nd (Black Watch), 78th (Ross-shire Buffs), 79th (Cameron Highlanders), 92nd (Gordon Highlanders) and 93rd (Sutherland Highlanders). The remaining five were line infantry regiments with Highland associations and wore trews instead of kilts – 72nd (Duke of Albany's Own), 73rd (Perthshire), 74th (Highland), 75th (Stirlingshire) and 91st (Argyllshire). In addition there were the Lowland regiments which wore standard British Army uniforms but were still identified as Scottish regiments. These were: 1st (Royal Scots), 21st (Royal Scots Fusiliers), 26th (Cameronians), 71st (Light Infantry) and 90th (Perthshire Light Infantry). By then Scotland also boasted a long-established cavalry regiment, the Royal Scots Greys, founded by General Tam Dalyell of the Binns in 1681, and the Scots Guards, raised in 1660.

Scottish regiments served in all of Wellington's campaigns in the first years of the 19th century and no Victorian skirmish was complete without the presence of at least one of their number. With their tartan uniforms and pipe bands, they became a distinctive group in the British Army as the Welsh or Irish were never to be, and in battle Highland soldiers were more noticeable, lending weight to the belief that they were better soldiers. 'They will praise the kilted regiment,' wrote a disgruntled private of the South Staffordshire Regiment from India. 'It's no use an English regiment trying to get on when there's a regiment with the kilts. The kilts put all the other regiments in the dark.' More significantly, perhaps, the kilted soldiers became a romantic cult, both for Royalty and for the rump of the civilian population who otherwise despised the army. Queen Victoria greatly admired her Highland soldiers and made a great fuss of the photographs taken of them by Roger Fenton at the Scutari military hospital during the Crimean War. In their grave bearded faces can be seen the epitome of what the public expected of the Scottish soldier: sternness in war and steadfastness in peace.

To an adoring public he was one of nature's gentleman – 'a lion in the field and a lamb in the house', or so the saying had it – and during the craze for joining the Volunteers, which was such an integral part of Victorian social life, Scottish recruitment was twice the national average. Certainly, in no other part of the country did the myth of the soldier put down deeper roots than in Scotland and the kilted 'Jock' became a very important figure indeed. In the days of his fame, after playing a decisive role at the Battle of Omdurman in 1898, Major-General Sir Hector Macdonald – popularly known as 'Fighting Mac' – warned his old civilian boss: 'Never let your employees lodge with soldiers or with those who were soldiers, for as sure as you do, you may look out to losing some of them.' The calling was as strong as that, and, in Macdonald's case, it had the added lure that he had risen from private to general, promotions almost unprecedented in the Victoria army.

In England, the reverse tended to be true. 'I shall name it to no one for I am ashamed to think of it,' wrote William Robertson's mother when he gave up the security of his family home in Lincolnshire in 1877 for the career of a trooper in the 16th Lancers. 'I would rather bury you than see you in a red coat.' Like Macdonald, Robertson went on to become an officer; later he became one of the army's greatest administrators, crowning his career with a field marshal's baton, but Mrs Robertson was not alone in showing such maternal concern for her son's choice of career. Countless other mothers fretted when their sons joined up and, until the Boer War in 1899, the army remained out of sight, though firmly in mind, fighting Queen Victoria's little wars of empire.

Scottish soldiers, though, were usually highly respected, if somewhat distant figures, and were considered to be so even if they were not of Scots origin but came from other parts of the British Isles. There was rarely a shortage of curious onlookers outside the gates of barracks, the arrival of troopships in Glasgow or Leith always attracted large crowds and military band concerts were a popular form of entertainment. Recruits were attracted for a number of obvious reasons, the uniform being one and the proud fighting conditions another. For many others, the poor, the dispossessed and the friendless, there was another impetus: soldiering in Scotland gave them the chance to serve in regiments which were more like families or clans than military units.

At the end of the Napoleonic wars, one of Wellington's generals, Sir David Stewart of Garth, was moved to say that the Scottish soldier stood apart from his fellows because 'he was taught to consider courage as the most honourable virtue, cowardice the most disgraceful failing'. Moreover, Stewart believed that the single reason why the Scottish soldier would display loyalty and steadfastness in combat was his membership of a particular regiment. Thus he could accept his own death, the wiping out of his company, even the annihilation of his own battalion, provided he was sure that the regiment would live on in the hearts of others. A century later, during the Rhine crossings in 1945, Major Martin Lindsay expressed a similar emotion when he claimed that his men never wavered in front of heavy German machine-gun fire because 'in the last resort, we were Gordon Highlanders, we were the Highland Division'.

The story of the Scottish soldier is a good one: the trouble was that the Scots swallowed it hook, line and sinker and added it to the panoply of myths which have surrounded the national psyche, usually to its detriment. For a start, many of the tartan-clad heroes who stare so pensively from innumerable Victorian prints and photographs were not even Scots by birth. Recent research has shown that just as the Swedish army rolls of the 17th century were thick with Scottish names, so too were the lists of many of Queen Victoria's Highland regiments filled with English or Irish soldiers. It has been estimated that by the 1870s only half of the officers and men in the Lowland regiments and the line regiments with Highland affiliations were actually Scots, and that in some, like the 73rd (Perthshire) Regiment, the Scots were outnumbered eight to one by the English and three to one by the Irish. (In 1881 this regiment was amalgamated with the predominantly Scottish 42nd to form the present-day Black Watch.) That being said, in the kilted Highland regiments during the same period the numbers of English rarely rose above 14 per cent and the Irish never above 3 per cent.

One of the reasons for the success of the Highland regiments in attracting recruits was undoubtedly the uniform, which had a turkey-cock allure outstripping anything else in the British Army, bar the cavalry and the Foot Guards. From head to toe, the average soldier in full fig made a brave sight – a tall bonnet mounted with black ostrich feathers, scarlet doublet with buff facings, accoutrements of a broadsword with basket hilt (for officers only after 1776), plaid, buckles and badges, and it is hardly surprising that Queen Victoria and her consort, Prince Albert, regarded the Highland regiments with special favour, for they seemed to epitomise their over-romanticised view of the Scottish Highlands and its people. If Walter Scott had much to answer for by creating this phenomenon, then the kilted figure of the Scottish soldier gave substance to the dream and helped to frame the myth. When Cardwell introduced his army reforms in 1881, and the regiments as we know them today came into being with territorial titles instead of numbers, the Lowland regiments took the opportunity to ape their northern cousins by introducing Highland-style uniforms, initially with a government tartan. As Stephen Wood has pointed out in his history of the Scottish soldier, there was a dreadful historical irony in the Lowlanders' desire to wear tartan: 'They lacked only the kilt and feather bonnet to resemble the sort of figure whose ancestors their ancestors despised, feared and slaughtered but who, in 1881, had come to personify Scotland.'

However, in full dress uniform the Scottish soldier was a figure who could hardly be ignored and he quickly made his presence felt in the world of advertising. Amongst the whisky blenders, Dewar's was one of the first to borrow the symbol and their pipe-major was as well known as the red-coated Johnnie Walker or Buchanan's black and white Highland terriers. To avoid possible repercussions from the regiments, the designers were careful to camouflage the uniform, but in his kilt, plaid and feathered bonnet, Dewar's mustachioed pipe-major could fit the bill of any Highland regiment – unlike some of the military figures used by the short-lived Pattisons of Leith, which went into receivership in 1898. Taking advantage of the late-Victorian craze for blended whisky – another by-product of the public passion for things Highland – Pattisons spent large sums of money promoting their 'wholesome, stimulating and creamlike' whisky and their advertisements made unashamed use of all too obvious, though crudely depicted, Scottish soldiers.

During the Second World War, Dewar's promoted a fine series of authentic drawings of Scottish soldiers from the different regiments to advertise their White Label blend in the United States and many of these became collectors' pieces. Buchanan's Black and White also found the British Army to be a happy hunting ground during the 1930s and their regimental series of advertisements offered an equally romantic view of the Scottish soldier. Blenders also borrowed regimental names to promote their wares and the following brands have appeared at various times during the 20th century: Black Watch (Robert Brown Ltd),

Cameron Highlander (Charles Mackinlay and Company), Cameronian Club (Robertson and Cameron), Gay Gordons (Gordon Campbell and Company), Highland Fusilier (Gordon and MacPhail), Royal Scot (George Dunlop and Company) and Scots Grey (Grey Rogers and Company). Although the King's Own Scottish Borderers have escaped this fate, like the Royal Highland Fusiliers, they have an exclusive blend produced for them by the Elgin firm of Gordon and MacPhail.

While the relationship between whisky and the Scottish regiments was undoubtedly good for marketing and advertising the product, there was a more serious connection, for Scottish soldiers had a reputation for hard drinking, especially during the Victorian period. Wellington had not been far wrong when he said that his soldiers were the scum of the earth, enlisted for drink. Drunkenness was common throughout the army and in some Scottish regiments the men were rarely sober – a parliamentary report into the nation's drinking habits, published in 1834, revealed that the Scots drank four gallons of whisky a year per head of adult population. Inevitably, the heavy drinking led to an increase in crime: drunkenness in public was not considered a punishable offence in civilian society but the military authorities cracked down on inebriated soldiers with considerable severity. Flogging was one remedy, and although it was not commonly employed by the mid-19th century, it was not finally abolished until 1881. In an attempt to curb drunkenness by less savage means, commanding officers were given the authority to fine their men in 1868. A year later War Office statistics revealed that 16 per cent of the army had been so punished. In 1876 it reached a peak of 28 per cent and even into the opening years of the 20th century, before the First World War, it was still a problem and the fine for a second offence was 2/6d, the equivalent for a private of two weeks' pay, less stoppages.

It was hardly surprising, perhaps, that the relationship between soldiers and hard drinking should also spawn a new mythology in popular folk-songs and even figure in the nation's literature. While the drunken dragoon or tipsy trooper is a stock figure of fun in many a broadside, with a folk heritage similar to the randy tinker, he had the same basis in fact as John Buchan's boozy Fusilier Jocks in *Mr Standfast* or James Kennaway's Scottish Jock Sinclair in *Tunes of Glory*, published in 1956. From the classic opening scene of the hard-drinking mess night to Sinclair's final mental collapse, copious draughts of whisky fuel the tragedy. (It is noticeable that Basil Barrow, Sinclair's rival for the command of the battalion, is mocked because he drinks brandy. 'We all drink whisky in this battalion,' Jock says when Barrow makes an unexpected appearance in the mess in the novel's opening pages.) Sinclair makes his intentions clear from the moment he is introduced by using whisky almost as a weapon with which to subjugate his men. 'Whisky. For the gentlemen that like it and for the gentlemen who don't like it, whisky.' Kennaway knew what he was talking about. As a National Service subaltern he had served with the Gordons in post-war Germany and with whisky costing 2½d a dram he had been shocked by the hard drinking and the fierce arguments which followed in the officers' mess.

None of these scenes, of course, ever found their way into the whisky producers' carefully manicured advertisements in which the officers invariably appeared as clean-limbed, square-jawed gentlemen with a twinkle in their eye, while the men were always stalwart, bewhiskered and distinctly martial. While it was useful to employ military symbolism in whisky advertisements and whisky became an ingredient in the army's own view of itself, the relationship between the distillers and blenders and the Scottish regiments was never as openly close as it was with the sporting world, another major source of promotion and, later, sponsorship. Snobbery was one reason and the regiments' natural reticence about their activities another. The former could be a powerful driving force in the lives of senior officers: for example, Field Marshal Earl Haig was thought to be acutely conscious of the fact that he was a 'Whisky Haig' and was associated, therefore, with trade, then considered to be an appalling solecism in the tightly knit world of the Edwardian upper classes and aristocracy. Certainly, his father's heavy drinking and outbursts of temper, the one fuelling the other, seem to have left Haig with a lifelong dislike of the effects of heavy drinking.

There was, though, one whisky magnate who was ostensibly proud of his relationship with the army and who made much of the fact that he preferred to employ soldiers from the Scottish regiments – Charlie Hepburn, who launched Red Hackle whisky in 1919 with the cap badge of the Black Watch as its main advertising symbol. In its heyday the blend was to be synonymous with the West of Scotland – unusual for a whisky associated with a regiment which recruits from Perthshire, Fife and Angus – but its blender was an all-Glasgow man who came to be one of the city's greatest philanthropists.

Charles Arthur Hepburn was born in Glasgow in 1891 and educated at Hillhead High School, where he was head boy and had a reputation of being a useful rugby player. After leaving school he worked for Peter Mackie's White Horse Distillers, while his brother, Brodie, was employed as a broker who eventually bought the Tullibardine Distillery and Deanston Distillery in Perthshire. On the outbreak of war, both brothers joined up, Brodie in the Black Watch and Charlie in the Royal Field Artillery. Wounded at the Battle of Neuve Chapelle in 1915, he also served on the Ypres sector and, after winning the Military Cross, transferred to the Black Watch with the rank of captain. There he met Corporal Joseph Ross, who also had experience of the whisky trade, having worked for the Bruichladdich Distillery on Islay, and after demobilisation they used their war gratuities to establish the firm of Hepburn & Ross and to launch the Red Hackle blend. It was an immediate success and Hepburn insisted that the advertising campaign should stress the close links with the armed forces – early advertisements included the statement that 'all members of the staff are ex-servicemen' and that the blend was 'a credit to their regiment'.

The campaign paid dividends. Then, as now, the Black Watch are perhaps Scotland's best-known regiment and they take great pride that they are the senior Highland regiment, able to trace their origins back to 1739 when they were formed as the Earl of Crawford's Regiment of Foot. Although considered suspect in some quarters because they were raised as a Hanoverian militia – others have called them a fine English regiment spoiled by a few Scotsmen – in many people's minds the Black Watch are *the* Scottish regiment and they are especially admired abroad. (Black Watch pipers played at the funeral service for John F. Kennedy.) Like other regiments, the Black Watch have their own peculiarities of uniform, the most recognisable being the dark government tartan which gave them their name, *Am Freiceadan Dubh*, or Black Watch. Another characteristic piece of dress is the prominent red hackle worn in the Tam o' Shanter in place of a cap badge. First granted to the regiment as an official piece of uniform in 1822, its origins are unknown, although early accounts of the Scottish regiments make mention of the 'red vulture feather' worn by the 42nd. What is certain is that the red hackle became closely associated with the Black Watch and that Hepburn hit on an instantly recognisable symbol for his new blend of whisky. Curiously, the regiment did not object to the association and allowed Hepburn & Ross to advertise the whisky in the pages of the regimental magazine called, unsurprisingly, *Red Hackle*.

Throughout the 1930s Red Hackle was considered to be a mature and smooth drinking blend, and from his Otago Street headquarters in Kelvinbridge, Hepburn built up a solid and profitable business. He also embarked on a second and more private career as an art collector and connoisseur, an interest which had been with him since childhood when as a five-year-old he had bought a pair of handcuffs reputedly used to take William Burke to the gallows in Edinburgh. In time, and as his fortune increased, so did Hepburn's tastes change and he became known in the art world as a serious collector of the works of Raeburn, Rembrandt, Reynolds and Ramsay. He was also interested in fine Persian and oriental carpets and his house in University Avenue in Glasgow soon became more of a gallery than a family home and was much visited by leading experts.

At the outbreak of the Second World War, Hepburn & Ross, like other blenders, had to face up to restrictions which allowed only short periods of distillings between then and 1944 and to the rationing of whisky, which was introduced in March 1940. Exports were allowed to continue and as Red Hackle had built up a following in the USA, Hepburn & Ross remained in a reasonably strong position throughout the war. However, the home market was by no means ignored and that proved to be Red Hackle's undoing. In the early months of the 'phoney war', Hepburn was one of the few optimists who believed that the war would soon be over, and that being so, he would be able to maintain his full quota of supplies to wholesalers under a government scheme which allowed them to purchase a percentage of the whisky they had received in the previous year. In the first year of operation, 1940–41, this was fixed at 41 per cent.

To begin with, Hepburn & Ross were able to maintain their standards as they had sufficient reserves, but as the war dragged on they were unable to fulfil their quotas and had to rely on filling from less reliable sources. Quality dropped and by 1945 Red Hackle was a shadow of its former self; in the austerity of the post-war years it was considered a poor choice and had become something of a joke in West of Scotland bars. Its reputation was not helped by unscrupulous publicans who used the ready availability of Red Hackle bottles to refill them with whatever was available – often the despised 'turnip juice' which had a black market sale during that period. In 1959 Hepburn decided to call it a day and sold out to the famous Glasgow firm of Robertson & Baxter, who, along with Highland Distillers, had supplied him with some of his best fillings. The selling price was reputed to be £2 million.

With his fortune Hepburn turned from collecting to philanthropy. In 1958, Glasgow University received his Raeburn painting of Stevenson McGill, Professor of Divinity, in memory of his wife Agnes. Glasgow Cathedral was presented with a fine collection of carpets and his old school was given £12,000 to provide a memorial gate and turnstiles for their playing fields at Hughenden. His most famous gift, though, was the purchase of an electric blanket for the Scottish Rugby Union's international stadium at Murrayfield in Edinburgh in 1959. Appalled by the fact that the season's international match against Wales had been threatened by heavy frosts, and that it had only been saved by the use of marquees and coke braziers, Hepburn asked GEC to come up with proposals for an underground electric blanket which would keep the playing surface frost-free throughout the winter. The SRU was approached and in time-honoured fashion hesitated before accepting Hepburn's generous offer. Murrayfield became the first international stadium to have this facility. Glasgow University eventually recognised Hepburn's philanthropy in 1964 when they awarded him the honorary degree of Doctor of Letters and he died in his Glasgow home on 16 July 1971. By then, few people remembered Red Hackle whisky and those who did, especially in Glasgow, recalled it with some mirth as a second-rate drink – a sorry fate for one of the city's great benefactors.

By then, too, the Scottish regiments had changed. Under the post-war reforms and reductions in defence spending, the Highland Light Infantry and the Royal Scots Fusiliers were amalgamated in 1959 to form the hybrid Royal Highland Fusiliers; they were followed in 1961 by a further amalgamation between the Cameron and Seaforth Highlanders to form the Queen's Own Highlanders, and in 1971 the Royal Scots Greys joined forces with the Carabiniers to form the Royal Scots Dragoon Guards. The two junior Lowland and Highland regiments, respectively the Cameronians and the Argyll and Sutherland Highlanders, were earmarked for disbandment in 1968, and while the former marched into history with great dignity, supporters of the Argylls mounted a noisy campaign which led to the regiment's reprieve, albeit initially at company level. At the time, the Argylls had captured the headlines through their high-profile approach to security duties in Aden and this undoubtedly helped their cause. The relationship between military and civilian society was also closer in the 1960s than it is today – many still youngish men had served in the forces during the war and others had done

National Service – and the people of Scotland still took a good deal of pride in their regiments.

By the 1970s, though, the gap between the armed forces and the rest of the nation had become much wider and the army had become once more a small and highly professional organisation, almost a caste apart. The reduction in military value of the reserve and territorial forces was another blow as throughout the Victorian period the Volunteers and Yeomanry had enjoyed huge popular support in Scotland. Indeed, in their exaggerated uniforms – often the product of a colonel's overheated romantic imaginings – they provided further evidence of national identity and were regarded by many Scots as a bulwark against the steady Anglicisation of Scottish life. With the emphasis on professionalism, though, reservists tended to wear the same drab olive battledress as the rest of the army and, due to the terrorist threat, serving soldiers no longer wore their uniforms in public places. In such an environment it is difficult to imagine any whisky producer following Hepburn's lead and launching a new blend based on the existing Scottish regiments. Would White Hackle (Royal Scots Fusiliers) or Blue Hackle (Queen's Own Highlanders) carry much significance for the market of the 21st century? I doubt it. A glimpse round the labels of today's blended whiskies confirms the triumph of the harsher climate of the Thatcherite 1980s when romance was out and realpolitik in. Even the bottles have changed to the smaller European measure, a move that would surely have induced Colonel Jock Sinclair to complain they were not a quarter empty but merely three-quarters full.

In no part of Britain did the myth of the Scottish soldier put down deeper roots than in Scotland and in no other part of the country does the family, or tribal, notion of the regiment hold sway. The Highlanders routing Cope at Prestonpans, the charge of the Scots Greys at Waterloo with the Gordons hanging on to the stirrups, the Thin Red Line of Sutherland Highlanders at Balaclava, the taking of the Atbara by the Camerons, the 15th Scottish Division at Loos, the 51st Highland Division at El Alamein, the Jocks in the Gulf: all these images spring out of history's pages to personify the nation at its most aggressive. For all these reasons, the defence cuts of 1991 were not only greeted with calls for the Scottish regiments to be spared, but also with the counter-charge that the Scottish soldier's cherished history and traditions had often been won in bloody battles or in subjugating innocent people and that such totems no longer had any place in late 20th-century life.

It was Clausewitz who said that the army was the mirror of the nation, which is another way of saying that soldiers are simply the rest of us in uniform. It is an adage which has particular relevance to Scotland for, if Clausewitz is correct, the Scottish soldier is at once a heroic and legendary figure, and a reminder of our own shortcomings.

In 1988 Arthur Bell & Sons initiated an advertising campaign on hoardings and in the colour supplements of the quality press which was of the greatest interest to students of how signs operate in society. The contents of each individual advertisement altered but the form remained constant – a kind of *trompe l'oeil* realism best exemplified by a certain tradition in American painting which reached its popular apotheosis in the work of Norman Rockwell. Each advert depicted a shelf cum bookcase (in one case a pinboard) carrying objects with Scottish associations: a Balmoral bonnet; antique copies of the Waverley novels; historic golf-balls of the period 1850 to 1905; an old Scots postcard; an antique microscope beside a copy of Sir Alexander Fleming's book on penicillin; part of the manuscript for Mendelssohn's overture *The Hebrides*; tickets for a Scotland versus France rugby match; the hilt of a claymore; and so on. The single recurrent item in each advert was a bottle of Bell's Extra Special Whisky.

The strategy of the campaign was clear. Bell's whisky was consistently located among objects which signified, most obviously, Scotland, but which also signified venerable old age, tradition and a certain kind of comfortable living, thereby transferring those qualities, by association, to the whisky itself. This cluster of meanings was enhanced by the advertisement being painted rather than photographed. While rendered in a highly realistic style, the advertisements, by bearing all the signs of the process of painting, were located in yet another discourse, that of high art, which reinforces the appeal to age and tradition.

What interested students of signification about the campaign was what could be called its semiotic overkill, its piling one on top of another of every conceivable emblem which might signify the conjunction of 'venerable' and 'Scottish'. Redundancy, the process of offering more channels of meaning than are strictly required for the message to be understood, is a feature of most sign systems, but seldom can redundancy have been carried further than in the Bell's campaign which corrals emblems from virtually every discourse within which, historically, Scotland and the Scots have been signified. Or, more accurately, the campaign pressed into service those discourses compatible with the conjunction venerable/Scottish/comfortable. Older and newer discourses about Scotland which might have troubled this conjunction are eschewed. The old narrative of Glasgow as 'the city of dreadful night', rehearsed in public health and urban planning literature, in novels and tabloid newspapers and, latterly, in films and television programmes, was clearly incompatible with the ideological thrust of the campaign, but so too was the newer narrative of Glasgow as commercially dynamic and upwardly mobile, perhaps because it lacked that element of venerable tradition so central to the campaign.

So familiar has the strategy become of linking particular products to imagined histories (e.g. Hovis and northern working-class life), and so widespread has it become with regard to Scotch whisky, that we might be forgiven for assuming that it has held sway unopposed since the marketing of Scotch whisky began. To think of whisky advertising is to think of the ensemble of images of Scotland deployed in the Bell's campaign. The historical actuality is, however, rather more complex. The whisky industry had displayed remarkable diversity and flexibility in its marketing strategies. To be sure, particular companies at particular moments have opted for one or other Scottish discourse in their advertising, but at other times, according to changes in the target audience or, in the argot of the trade, product placement, they have been prepared to abandon the Scottish national discourse for the wider *British* national discourse and to abandon both for other discourses, most notably that of social class.

There is a debate among historians about the vexed question of historical time. The dominant practice (certainly among historians in the English-speaking world) has been to construct the past into periods (the Ancient World, the Classical World, the Dark Ages, the Renaissance, etc) with a tendency to view these constructs as hermetically sealed from each other. A rather more sophisticated view would see events and institutions as existing in several historical times simultaneously. For instance, a French economic historian has described the outbreak of the French Revolution in 1789 as a fusion of three separate times: a long time (the economic expansion of the 18th century); a medium time (the recurrent economic depressions of 1774–88); and a short time (the price crisis of 1789). Some such model of the interlacing of long-, medium-, and short-term discourses is necessary to understand the extremely complex history of the marketing of Scotch whisky. Several discourses are often present simultaneously. In the Bell's campaign, for example, as well as the dominating discourses of *nation* and *class*, there are to be found the discourse of *high art* (in the actual form of the adverts and the reference to Mendelssohn) and a Scottish variant of the *biography* discourse – Great Scots. Five minutes in any Scottish library or bookshop will confirm the suffocating omnipresence of this hagiographic strain in our national life.

The most surprising feature of early whisky advertising, in the 50 years or so before the First World War, was its diversity. It was not dominated, as might be supposed, by images of Scotland. Although such images were not absent, one has the impression that they were simply part of an extremely wide range of discourses drawn upon to sell the product. Those adverts which did deploy Scottish motifs often opted for one of two images: the Highlander, whether in his romantic or comic dimension, and Scottish soldiers in the British Army, an inflection of the romantic motif in which the supposed warlike qualities of the Scots are evoked. However, such images in early whisky advertising are in a minority. It comes as no surprise that the oldest, folkloric idea about whisky, its alleged health-giving properties, is pressed into service. More surprisingly, we find whisky advertising of this period deploying images as varied as a naval ironclad, Father Christmas, Chelsea pensioners, English law courts and Japanese prints.

The development of the mass market, and therefore of

advertising, in the last third of the 19th century coincided with a specific opportunity for Scotch whisky to enlarge its market. Up till the 1880s brandy and gin, both of them socially superior to whisky, had been the main spirits drunk by the English. The English upper classes had increasingly encountered whisky on their sojourns to the Scottish Highlands in the wake of Queen Victoria's imprimatur on the area. Whisky had hitherto been seen as a robust, outdoor drink with perhaps some health-giving qualities, but it had an unfortunate association with the lower orders and therefore was quite unsuitable for club or salon. The devastation of the continental brandy trade in the 1880s due to *phylloxera* gave Scotch whisky the opportunity to make inroads into the club and salon market. But for this to succeed two factors were necessary: whisky's robustness had to be tempered by blending and it had to be constructed ideologically as a proper beverage for more refined milieux. This construction of whisky's *class* discourse began to be apparent in its marketing, becoming an increasingly dominant motif across diverse brands and establishing itself as one of the long-term discourses associated with the product, as is apparent in Bell's campaign referred to above.

The central discourse of that campaign was of course longevity and tradition. This became established quite early in whisky advertising. Haig had the edge on its competitors, having some claim to be the oldest whisky-maker, which was exploited in its marketing. It celebrated 1927 as its tercentenary and its advertising in that year referred back to the way various things were done in the year 1627. Significantly, and perhaps somewhat surprisingly, the campaign did not deploy Scottish motifs. Other brands were forced to suggest their longevity by more connotative means, as in Dewar's campaign of the turn of the century which presented the firm's name chiselled in stone with historical and even archaeological associations. Although the organising discourse of both the Haig and the Dewar campaigns is Age/Tradition, there is a formalist discourse present, that of repetition: in the case of the Dewar campaign, stone carving; in the Haig case, disparate events of 1627. Indeed, it could be said that repetition is marketing's formalist discourse *par excellence*, the recurrent identifying feature which gives the idea of 'campaign' meaning.

As the marketing of Scotch whisky developed, so did its deployment of a cluster of discourses signifying Scotland and indissolubly linking the product to its place of origin, to the extent that, faced with the Bell's campaign of the 1980s/'90s, we tend to think of the link as natural rather than constructed in history.

The representation of Scotland and the Scots had risen in importance over two centuries, much encouraged by the Ossian episode in the 18th century and by Queen Victoria's association with the Highlands in the 19th century. But those events were themselves symptoms of a long historical process, dating from the mid-18th century, whereby Scotland became, for European pre-Romantics and Romantics, a delirious realm of the imagination in which the land itself, peopled by a noble race of bards, warriors and winsome lasses, exercised a magical, transformative sway over any who came there.

A constructed identity was imposed on the land and people of Scotland which to a large extent they have come to live within. The process was not dissimilar to that visited on other peripheral peoples in their encounters with European imperialism (e.g. the Polynesians, the Africans, the Arabs, etc) as has been set out in the writings of Franz Fanon and Edward Said, among others.

This discourse, with its cluster of motifs and its

accretions and contradictions (e.g. the comic versus the romantic Scot) was deployed in every conceivable sign system (novels, paintings, operas, ballets, postcards, films, television programmes); not least in the marketing of Scotch whisky. The Scottish discourses deployed in whisky selling were not wholly static and repetitive. Certain images of the Scots present in early whisky advertising became less and less apparent, most notably the parsimonious and, in particular, the drunken Scot. As the discourses of Class and Heritage became increasingly important in whisky advertising, they merged in the figure of that modern centaur who is Scot from the waist down and English gentleman from the waist up. He, above all, is the icon who represses and displaces the rumbustious drunkard as whisky climbs the social ladder. The drunken Scot, with his cousin the miserly Scot, continued to stalk other sectors of representation, particularly the Scottish comic postcard. Here could be found the demented *doppelgänger* of the refined Anglo-Scottish gentleman languidly or heartily raising his glass in the whisky adverts. The shelves and pinboards of Bell's 1980s campaign are assuredly not those of this deranged Mr Hyde. Indeed, it would be an amusing exercise to redesign the Bell's campaign to appeal to the drunken proletariat. Instead of a teak bookcase, a clumsily erected MFI chipboard one; instead of two tickets for the Scotland *v* France rugby game, two tickets to a Rangers *v* Celtic cup-tie; instead of first editions of Burns and Scott, a paperback version of *No Mean City* and a video cassette of *Take the High Road*; instead of 'Fingal's Cave' overture, the sheet music of Andy Stewart's 'A Scottish Soldier'; instead of a piece of fine, antique Scottish silver, a ceramic, tartan-tammied Scotty bearing the words 'A wee gift frae Dunoon', and so on. Although the discourses of Class, Age/Tradition and Scotland were to become long-term and dominant as the marketing of Scotch whisky developed, another long-term discourse came to be deployed which is best described as Formalism in the sense that it emerges from the structure of language and narrative itself. An early example of the formalist discourse is Buchanan's marketing their brand Black & White round the structural opposition of these colours. Discourses are rather like Chinese boxes or Russian dolls in that one may lie within several others. It is clear that when the Buchanan black and white opposition was deployed in relation to people it would abut on ideas of racism and imperialism, themselves discourses in the process of construction in the late 19th century. As time passed, the Buchanan opposition increasingly centred on the black and white Scotch terriers which became a trademark for the brand. A similar structural opposition central to narrative, that between Then and Now, Past and Present, informed a Johnnie Walker campaign of the late 1940s. Although Bell's in recent years have marketed within an archetypically Scottish discourse (imbricated, of course, with other discourses such as Class) for a long time their marketing relied on the formalist device of the pun on their own name, a device also extensively deployed by Teacher's.

Whisky, in common with other products (increasingly so in the 'Heritage' context of the British society), has often geared its marketing round particular historical figures. To restate the point that whisky's marketing has historically extended far beyond images of Scotland, it is probable that the main historical figures used have not been Scots (e.g. Queen Anne, William IV, George IV). However, the main Scottish historical personages who have figured in the marketing of Scotch whisky are particularly interesting: Drambuie's Charles Edward Stuart; Highland Queen's Mary, Queen of Scots; and

Chivas Regal's Robert the Bruce. Significantly, the dominant, popular narratives of Mary and Charles Edward are associated with tragedy and loss, exemplifying the romantic pessimism, the sentimental wallowing in ill-fortune, which is such a disabling feature of so much Scottish life and art. Associated with the use of royal figures is the other discourse, common to many peripheral countries, of celebrating the 'great men' the society has produced. This was particularly deployed by Dewar's in their pre-First World War campaign, Famous Scots, reproductions of a series of portraits of figures such as Charles Edward Stuart, Sir Walter Scott, Sir Harry Lauder and many others, which Dewar's commissioned from contemporary artists.

It is something of a cliché that British culture is primarily literary and dramatic rather than orientated to the visual arts. This certainly seems to be confirmed by the forays that the marketing of Scotch whisky has made into British culture. Johnnie Walker ran an extensive campaign in the pre-First World War period which was structured round English popular songs. When whisky marketing has turned to high culture the terrain has been dominated by those giants of British culture, Shakespeare and Dickens. Dewar's ran a campaign in the 1920s round the slogan 'The spirit of . . .' illustrating such ideas as Friendship, Humour and Hope by reference to Shakespearean characters. Buchanan's ran a campaign during the First World War round the characters of Dickens' novels and Justerini and Brooks used images of Dickens himself in one of their American campaigns of the 1960s.

What is, of course, particularly interesting here is that Scotch whisky has primarily deployed *British* rather than *Scottish* culture in its marketing, Dickens and Shakespeare rather than Burns and Scott, *English* rather than *Scottish* popular song. This does not mean that figures such as Burns and Scott have been entirely repressed. One can hear resonances of Scott in the brand named The Antiquary, although its advertising does not make the connection explicit. However, this provides further evidence that historically speaking, our impression that the marketing of Scotch whisky is wholly bound up with images of Scotland is probably mistaken.

As has been noted, one of the earliest motifs in the very diverse ensemble of marketing strategies deployed by the whisky trade was the image of the Highland soldier. On closer inspection, however, this was often part of a non-specific discourse of *militarism.* This was so in the colourful campaign run by Buchanan's in the mid-1930s which made reference to a whole range of regiments of the British Army, only some of which were Scottish. However, the tradition of deploying warlike Highlanders in whisky advertising was notably continued in a campaign run by Dewar's in the United States in the early 1940s both before and after the entry of the United States to the war. This campaign, which linked Dewar's own winning of awards at international trade fairs to battle honours won by Scottish regiments, may have represented a discreet linking of commerce and patriotism.

It has been suggested that the discourses of Age/Tradition, of Formalism, and of Scotland constitute the deep-seated and recurrent long-term discourses within which Scotch whisky has been marketed and that medium- and short-term discourses have also entered the field. One of the most powerful discourses at play within British society, particularly in the period 1880 to 1945, was imperialism. The marketing strategies of whisky were less prone to deploy this than were the strategies of many other products (e.g. tobacco, rubber) whose raw materials originated in the (then) colonies. It would be gratifying, if rather wishful, to think that Scotch whisky's reluctance to play the imperialist card was due to the industry's recognition of the internal colonial status of Scotland within the British state. However, as several of the essays in this volume make clear, the Scotch whisky industry and its barons were more than complicit with that state and its imperial pretensions. Indeed, on the occasions when imperialism did appear in whisky advertising it was no less inhibited than elsewhere, as in Dewar's 'Spirit of the Empire' campaign of the 1920s. However, other brands deployed imperialist images (no less aggressively). Dewar's pre-eminence in this regard is perhaps best summed up in its 1937 image of John Bull raising a glass of White Label.

To categorise discourses as long-, medium- and short-term is a convenient analytic tool, but it has its limitations. Is imperialism a long- or a medium-term discourse? Also, a long-term discourse can be 'cashed' as a short-term one as in the case of the Peter Dawson campaign of 1924 which is structured round the Empire Exhibition of that year at Wembley.

Unquestionably, the two world wars constitute short-term discourses and it is very instructive to compare the terms in which Scotch whisky was marketed in both wars. As befits the difference in tone in Britain's attitudes to the First World War and the Second World War, and the differing public rhetoric which flowed from them, the wartime marketing campaigns for Scotch whisky were quite different from one war to the other. Johnnie Walker's jingoistic campaign of 1914–15 may have been of a piece with other events in British society of that time, such as handing out white feathers and smashing shops with German names. It is certainly more breast-beating and xenophobic than the campaigns by the same brand and by VAT 69 in the Second World War.

The most short-term of all discourses deployed in the marketing of Scotch whisky are those relating to specific, concrete, historical moments. These cover diverse events: the Royal Jubilee of 1935 (Dewar's); the flu epidemic of 1936 (Dewar's); the wartime pact among Britain, the USA and the Soviet Union (Dewar's); the 1951 Festival of Britain (Dewar's); the 1953 Coronation (VAT 69); and the 1964 opening of the Forth Road Bridge (King George IV).

This essay has sought to examine the popular perception that the marketing of Scotch whisky is dominated by images of Scotland. While such images have been present from the start, have developed into one of the most central discourses within which Scotch whisky presents itself to the world, and may now constitute the dominant images, this has not always been so. Scotch whisky has deployed a rich variety of discourse historically, most of them not specific to Scotland. Where it has adopted images of Scotland, these have been highly selective, tending to the rural and the kitsch, repressing the urban and the contradictory, and invariably interpenetrated with other hegemonic discourses such as Class. As nationhood moves further up the agenda of world politics, this process is unlikely to be reversed.

The scene is 'a most excellent inn' in Inveraray and the date is 23 October 1773. Boswell and Johnson, on the return leg of their Hebridean tour, have 'supped well' and after supper, reported Boswell, 'Mr Johnson, whom I had not seen taste any fermented liquor before or during our expedition, had a gill of whisky brought to him. "Come," said he, "let me know what it is that makes a Scotsman happy." He drank it all but a drop, which I begged leave to pour into my glass, that I might say we had drank whisky together.' (This is the version in Boswell's original manuscript: the published version, incorporating suggested 'improvements' by Boswell's friend and helper the scholar Edmund Malone, has 'Dr Johnson' and 'Scotchman'.)

So, clearly, already in 1773 whisky was known in

England as the drink that 'makes a Scotsman happy'. The music-hall song that was popular nearly a century and a half later, after the price of whisky had risen from four shillings to twelve and sixpence a bottle, asked 'How can a fellow be happy, if happiness costs such a lot?' One might ask how whisky makes a fellow happy. It is one thing to believe that whisky makes a contribution to the good life, which for centuries it did in Scotland as wine has done in France; it is quite another to consider it as an escape from a life of squalor and impoverishment, as it increasingly became in Scotland's industrial cities, notably Glasgow, in periods of depression. One suspects that the music-hall happiness had little in common with that referred to by Dr Johnson.

There are two extremes between which the view of the function of whisky in Scotland has swung: on the one hand, a product of the country produced by a cottage industry that was a natural part of the farmer's year, and on the other a road to euphoria and even oblivion, a road taken by comic drunken Scots in kilts with slurred speech and double vision. The dichotomy is apparent from at least the 18th century.

> A distillery, on a pretty extensive scale, was lately erected near Aberdeen; it was completed on the 29th September 1794. The chief inducement for erecting it there was the command of water, 38 feet perpendicular upon the banks of a navigable river. It was intended to distil annually the produce of 12,000 quarters of corn (i.e. barley), but could do much more . . . The principal part of the corn grew in Aberdeenshire: the rest was imported from adjacent districts. The whole was the growth of Scotland.

This is from 'the communication of several gentlemen' of Aberdeen published in volume XIX of *The Statistical Account of Scotland*, 1797. The great pride in the distillery and the recognition that it played a part in Scotland's economy can be contrasted with what appears in volume XI of the *Statistical Account*, 1794, in a contribution by the Reverend Mr Archibald Robertson, minister of the parish of Kildalton, Islay.

> This island hath a liberty of brewing whisky, without being under the necessity of paying the usual excise duty to government. We have not an excise officer in the whole island. The quantity therefore of whisky made here is very great; and the evil that follows drinking to excess of this liquor, is very visible in this island. This is the chief cause of our poverty, for the barley that should support the family of the poor tenant, is sold to a brewer for 17s. the boll; and the same farmer is often obliged to buy meal at £1.3s. Sterling, in order to keep his family from starving.

Against this we can set the testimony of the Reverend Mr Alexander Stewart, minister of the parish of Moulin in Perthshire, who wrote in volume V of the *Statistical Account*, 1793, that in spite of two licensed stills in the parish and 30 licensed retailers of ale, beer and whisky, the people consumed their liquor wisely.

> Even at weddings, and on holidays, instances of persons drinking to excess are few, and a drunken squabble is extremely rare. It is somewhat remarkable, that among people who hardly know how to make a bargain, or pay a debt, except over a dram of whisky, moderation should be so

> generally observed; particularly when it is considered that at the fairs, every house, hut and shed in the respective villages is converted into a dram-shop.

An even more positive account of the place of whisky is given by the Reverend Mr David Dunoon in the parish of Killearnan in Ross-shire in volume XIII of the *Statistical Account*, 1796:

> It will be asked, why then so many distilleries? For these reasons: distilling is almost the only method of converting our victual into cash for the payment of rent and servants; and whisky may, in fact, be called our staple commodity. The distillers do not lay the proper value on their time and trouble, and of course look on all, but the price of barley and fire added to the tax, as clear profit; add to these the luxury of tasting the quality of the manufacture during the process.

One could go on quoting indefinitely on both sides of the question – whisky is a good social drink and a benefit to the local economy, or it is a cause of dissipation and poverty – but it is after the rise of blended whisky in the 19th century, and of the big firms that produced and marketed it, that we get the condescending myth of the drunken music-hall Scot. Of course, any alcoholic spirit is liable to abuse, but if it is a local product that arises naturally from the interplay of local resources and the rhythms of local life, the positive side is more visible and 'what makes a Scotsman happy' is not what makes him into a drunken sot. Elizabeth Grant, of Rothiemurchus, in her *Memoirs of a Highland Lady 1797–1827*, gives some vivid glimpses of the drinking of whisky by all social classes as part of the normal rhythm of life, beginning when new-born infants were given a spoonful to start them properly on their journey through life.

Even in the age of the great whisky entrepreneurs of the late 19th century, however, when whisky as a cottage industry had been decisively transformed into whisky as big business, it was possible to see whisky and its production as a natural part of the Scottish scene. Alfred Barnard, in his marvellously attractive book on the whisky distilleries of Britain, first published in 1887, gives us happy pictures of Scottish distilleries in their local setting that makes us think of whisky production as an integral and healthy part of the Scottish landscape. The opening of his chapter on Lagavulin Distillery, Islay, illustrates this nicely:

> From Ardbeg, our route homeward lay through the beautiful village of Lagganmhouillin or Lagavulin, 'the Mill in the Valley', and no prettier or more romantic spot could have been chosen for a distillery. We trotted merrily along, the horse apparently knowing that its face was stable-ward, and the driver, evidently anticipating another 'wee drappie' at our next halting place, occasionally broke out into song, but as it was in Gaelic we were none the wiser, and his command of the English language was so limited that he could not favour us with a translation.

Far from sharing the ecclesiastical disapproval of whisky shown by the Reverend Mr Archibald Robertson in 1794, Barnard saw church and distillery as bound up in a common local bond:

> Close to the Distillery, as if to throw round the establishment its spirited protection, stands a

> quaint-looking church; the bell which summons the worshippers instead of being in the tower, is fixed on a cross-tree of pyramidical shape on the top of a neighbouring hill, so that its sound may reach the remotest parts of the parish. The clergyman's residence, like the church, is picturesquely situated beside a rocky inlet of the sea coast . . . On reaching the village we put the horses up and proceeded to inspect the Distillery.

Barnard made his pilgrimage to the distilleries in the heyday of the whisky industry's expansiveness. It all began with the invention of a new kind of still in 1830 by Aeneas Coffey, formerly Inspector-General of Excise in Ireland. This 'patent still' was designed for the production of a spirit from a mixture of malted and unmalted barley mashed with other cereals (as distinct from the traditional pot-still whisky made from malted barley only): the distillation process was continuous, and thus much cheaper than distillation in the pot-still, and it could use virtually any kind of grain – or indeed other substances too. The patent-still whisky derived no peaty flavour from peat-dried malt nor did it contain the oils and other aromatic substances that give the product of each malt whisky its individual flavour, but by blending it with a smaller proportion of malt whiskies one could produce an acceptable drink at much less cost than malt whisky and furthermore a drink that could be diluted with soda water or other liquids without criminal damage. The great pioneers of blended Scotch whisky – the Haigs, the Dewars, the Walkers, James Buchanan, the Mackies (White Horse) and William Sanderson (VAT 69) were also pioneers in brash advertising and made blended Scotch whisky into a world drink. By the 1890s the production of blended Scotch whisky was getting out of control, and after the spectacular crash of the whisky firm of Pattison's

Limited (which used in their advertising hundreds of grey parrots trained to cry, on being released, 'Drink Pattison's whisky') in 1898, the pace slowed down.

The association of distillers known as the Distillers Company Ltd (now United Distillers) kept a careful eye on new developments in the industry with a view to avoiding disasters associated with over-production. But at the end of the 19th century there was still something exciting and romantic about Scotch whisky, even though whisky-and-soda was becoming the gentleman's drink (ladies did not drink whisky until much later) and the drinker of a pot-still single malt whisky was likely to be an eccentric connoisseur like Professor George Saintsbury. Whisky had become part of the romantic Highlands syndrome, and joined the stream of influences that stemmed first from Scott's *Lady of the Lake* and then his *Waverley* and later from Queen Victoria's establishing herself at Balmoral and showed Scotland as a romantic land of mist and mountains. (The fact that *Waverley* is actually an anti-romantic novel need not detain us here: it was the popular image that mattered.) There was an aristocratic element here too, deriving not only from Queen Victoria's Balmoral but from sporting estates and the image of tweedy and/or kilted sportsmen hunting, shooting and fishing in their Scottish playground with their silver flasks of whisky always available to provide refreshment. (I remember when I was a young man being taken out trout fishing on a private loch by a wealthy sportsman who had a special whisky flask available so that each fish caught could be suitably toasted as soon as it was landed.) The *phylloxera* infestation that devastated the Cognac vineyards in the 1880s encouraged the movement from brandy to whisky (and, on the sideboards of country-house dining-rooms, from brandy-and-soda to whisky-and-soda) and gave another aristocratic image to the whisky trade.

Blended whisky, however, remained cheap until the First World War and became the working man's Friday or Saturday night drink on which he spent often a large proportion of his week's pay. In the famous words of the Will Fyffe song:

> I'm only a common auld working man
> As anyone here can see,
> But when I get a couple of drinks on a Saturday
> Glasgow belongs to me!

A strange blend of Highland stereotypes, music-hall humour (Harry Lauderism) and that Scottish self-contempt which seems to be a feature of a nation uncertain of its identity projected the whisky-drinking Scot as an international figure of fun. And, just as it was the Aberdonian who provided most of the jokes about the alleged Aberdonian stinginess, it was the Scots who created this figure.

The scene has changed in recent times in various ways. Whisky is no longer cheap even in relative terms, and it is not, as it was in Scotland before the First World War, a significant working-class drink. 'A nip an' a pint' or 'a hauf an' a hauf' are not phrases now heard in Edinburgh or Glasgow. And though the lemonade bottle still appears on a few pub counters, the drinking of whisky and lemonade, for long a working-class habit, has almost died out. (The origin of this damnable combination has never been clear to me, but I have long suspected that it is a degenerate descendant of the 18th-century whisky punch made with whisky, sugar, hot water and lemon juice.) The actual production of whisky goes on very much as it has done for a long time, with malt distilleries and grain distilleries both flourishing, though a few have ceased production. The trade, however, is no longer in the hands of family firms, except for a few isolated instances. The big men of finance and multiple internationals have moved in, and although they have not interfered with the traditional way of making pot-still malt whisky to any significant degree, the whole structure of the industry is now a network of interlocking financial and industrial interests, with Canadian, American, French and Japanese firms involved, that baffles the ordinary whisky drinker or even the connoisseur interested in the taste and quality of the product. And such connoisseurs are, paradoxically enough, steadily growing in numbers. Twenty years ago drinkers of single malt whisky were few and far between, and it was only in a few pubs and hotels that one could be certain of getting a dram of the true malt. Now single malts, though representing only a small proportion of whisky bottled and sold, are readily available all over the country as well as in America and on the continent of Europe. (I have seen a window full of single malts in a shop in Venice and an enormous collection of different malts in a liquor supermarket in San Francisco.)

The entrepreneurs and money men have not had it all their own way. Just as the campaign for real ale forced brewers to revive traditional cask-conditioned beer, so a succession of books and articles on Scotch whisky stressing the significance of the individual single malts, each with its unique flavour, have educated a generation in the true nature and quality of the original pot-still malt whisky. People are actually drinking whisky for its nose and taste and not as a short-cut to synthetic 'happiness'.

In 1935 Neil Gunn produced his classic book, *Whisky and Scotland*. This was a fiercely polemical work, attacking the fictions about Scotch whisky put about by the blenders, deploring grain or patent-still whisky, and passionately defending the single malts. My own discovery of this work was the beginning of my education in whisky. The effect of the book was not immediate, but slowly it made its way into the consciousness of a number of Scots drinkers and slowly the revival of the single malt as the true Scotch whisky began to get under way. If we were to ask ourselves today what Gunn's title *Whisky and Scotland* would mean in terms of deposition of both whisky and of Scotland, what would we say?

We would have to point to the ambivalence of the tradition of whisky drinking in Scotland that has existed at least since the 18th century and show its relation to moral, religious, social, economic and cultural factors. We would have to explain the whole tradition of exciseman versus private distiller that provided one of the earliest Scottish myths about whisky: the cunning illicit distiller, pursuing his God-given right to distil his own grain, versus the wicked revenue man. We would have to explore the significance of whisky as a freedom symbol ('Freedom and whisky gang thegither'). We would have to look at the impact of the Act of 1823 that provided more lenient terms for legal distillers and so encouraged men like George Smith of Glenlivet to 'go legitimate' in 1824, to be followed by other previously illicit distillers. We would have to examine the impact of the great whisky entrepreneurs of the latter part of the 19th century and of their advertising. We would have to examine the use of whisky by hopeless men and women in city slums and the powerful prohibitionist movement that grew up as a result. Then of course there is the Harry Lauderism movement I have discussed, whisky and the stage Scot, the picture-postcard Highlander with the bottle of whisky stuck in his kilt, as well as the very different image of whisky and the sporting aristocrat. In our time, there is the recovery of the taste for single malt whiskies, with *discrimination* (both to the nose and the palate) as the important matter, coinciding paradoxically with the ownership of the whisky trade by vast complexes of international industry.

At the end of it all, we could not avoid the political dimension. The history of the part whisky has played in the picture of Scotland as seen by the world (and for that matter as seen in Scotland too) is bound up with the Scot's image of himself, which is the image he exports. And that image is largely conditioned by the political reality of Scottish life and endeavour. The Scot as joke-character for the amusement of the English and others, like the comic Negro of earlier American humour, is a reflection of something real in the state of Scotland and her people. And yet – is it not a cultural rather than a political situation we are involved with? Or perhaps the two cannot be separated? Perhaps education is the answer: would not properly diffused historical knowledge be helpful in substituting reality for stereotypes? To know and understand the social, economic and cultural forces that have shaped the Scot's self-image, and to set this beside the actual facts of the production and marketing of whisky and to see the reflection of all this in our literature and folklore, is to know the score in Scotland. Hugh MacDiarmid's remarkable poem-sequence, *A Drunk Man Looks at the Thistle,* is the great counter-statement to the music-hall tradition about the Scot and whisky. Perhaps every Scot should at some stage in his education be asked to meditate on the cultural significance of whisky in the work of, say, Robert Fergusson, Robert Burns, Hugh MacDiarmid and Compton Mackenzie. If *Whisky Galore* is funny (and it is), why? And is this a Good Thing?

Some things don't change: bucolic tradition, mostly imaginary, as a means of selling whisky.

Iconic Scottishness identifies the product: kilt, tartan, sporran and bagpipes.

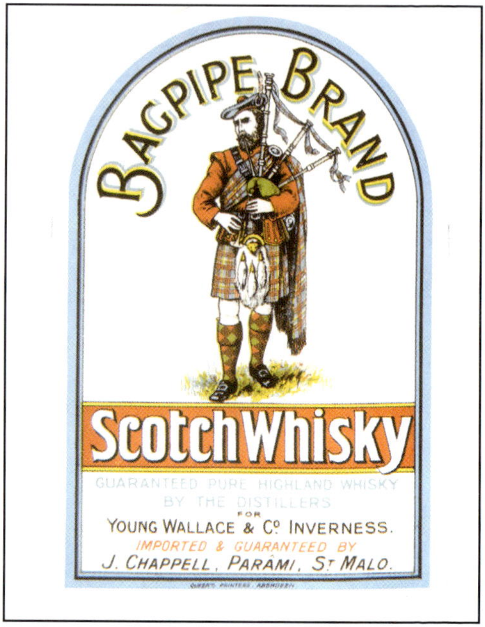

The kilt now with (respectable) tweed jacket and (faithful) attendant dog – and whisky identified with traditional hospitality.

Laying it on thick: Bell's associated with literacy (books), science (microscope), engineering (locomotive) etc.

Laying it on thick again: Bell's associated with golf (golf balls), the military (Glengarry bonnet, sword-hilt), agriculture (steer, rosette), craftsmanship (wooden quaich).

The imagery adapted for the colonies: a Highland landscape for the Indians – together with most un-Scottish-looking trees.

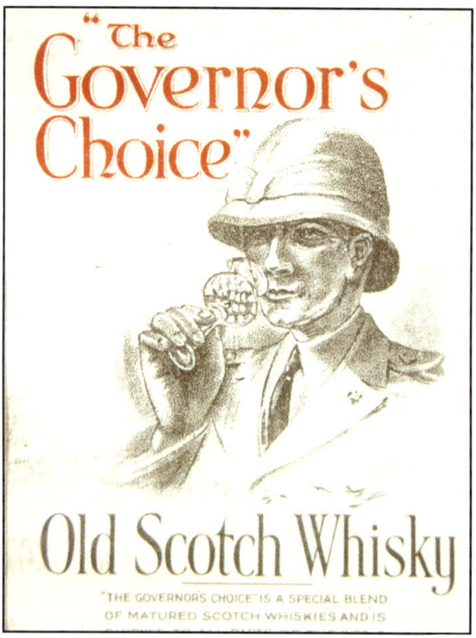

More imperial than colonial. The gent in the sunhat looks suitably stern – possibly because of the difficulty of drinking from a glass shaped like a thistle.

Drink for the diaspora: Burns's enthusiasm for the ideals of the French Revolution was suitably adapted. Fraternity was OK, Liberty and Equality conveniently forgotten.

Whisky as a drink for the upper classes. Chap in full military rig contemplating an extremely large and un-Scottish-looking castle.

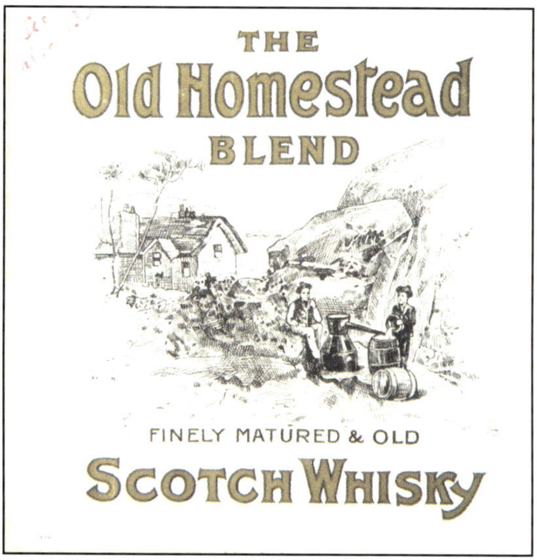

Whisky as a drink for the upper classes. Peasant origins make whisky acceptable to an industrial age.

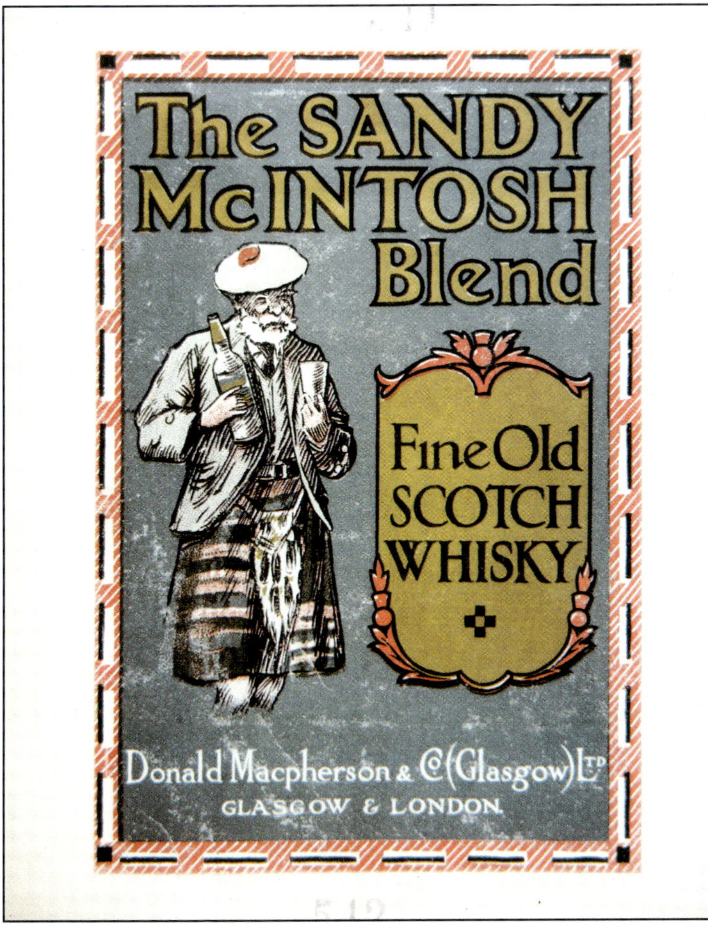

Tartan and kilts becoming kitsch: whisky's debt to the music hall.

Whisky becomes British.

A version of Scottish imagery evidently created by someone who knew nothing of the originals – and note the address: NB stands for North Britain, a designation for people who thought the term 'Scotland' somewhat disloyal.

Thae curst horse-leeches o' th' Excise,
Wha make the Whisky still their prize!
Haud up thy han' Deil! ance, twice, thrice!
  There, seize the blinkers!
An' bake them up in brunstane pies
  For poor damn'd Drinkers.

Exciseman Robert Burns, *Scotch Drink*

'The Highlander . . . is beginning to feel that the exploitation of his whisky is a parable for the exploitation of much else.'

Exciseman Neil Gunn, *Whisky and Scotland*

A few years before he died, Sir Compton Mackenzie summoned me for an audience at his home in 31 Drummond Place, Edinburgh. It was 1969 and Mackenzie was then 86, the Grand Old Man of Scottish Letters; I was 60 years younger, and a young man trying to make my way in literary Scotland. Apprehensive at meeting such a kenspeckle character, I fortified myself beforehand with a quarter bottle of Bell's, not appreciating the difference between blended whisky, the hard stuff, and malt whisky, the smooth stuff. I arrived and Mackenzie put me at ease with a drop of the soft stuff, Talisker I think it was, and I noticed the difference, feeling a warm glow engulf me as he talked about his eventful life; a sensation quite unlike the bolt from the quarter bottle of Bell's.

Mackenzie took himself seriously as a writer, not surprisingly since his early novel *Sinister Street* (1913) was acclaimed as masterly by critics of the calibre of Ford Madox Ford and Henry James. He took Scotland seriously too in his epic sequence *The Four Winds of Love* (1937–45), which features a fictional superman, John Ogilvie, who discovers his Scottish roots in Assynt and hopes to preside over a Scotland renewed by a rediscovery of its Celtic culture. Alas, readers did not respond to the *Four Winds* as Mackenzie hoped they would. They preferred the farcical Mackenzie, the man who made fun of Scotland in comic novels, especially *Whisky Galore* (1947).

Written in English but drawing on the time he lived in the Outer Isles, *Whisky Galore* is a satirical salute to the thirst of the Todday islanders who, finding themselves in wartime deprived of their usual dram, react hysterically (and hilariously) when they learn that the SS *Cabinet Minister* is wrecked off Little Todday with a cargo of whisky. It is raided as a treasure of 'liquid gold' but is not the malt whisky traditionally distilled in the Highlands and Islands. It is (and Mackenzie based the story on the wreck of the SS *Politician*, in 1941 off Eriskay, with 2,000 cases of Haig and Haig) blended whisky, as Mackenzie makes clear in his catalogue of names:

> Beside the famous names known all over the world by ruthless and persistent advertising for many years, there were many blends of the finest quality . . . There was Highland Gold and Highland Heart, Tartan Milk and Tartan Perfection, Bluebell, Northern Light, Preston Pans, Queen of the Glens, Chief's Choice and Prince's Choice, Islay Dew, Silver Whistle [and so on and so on] and the glass of every bottle was stamped with a notice which made it clear that whisky like this was intended to be drunk in the United States of America and not by the natives of the land where it was distilled, matured and blended.

Blended whisky is the dram Mackenzie puts into the drama that disturbs the life of the islanders. Though the novel is intended as light literary relief, Mackenzie makes a poignant point in showing the islanders dependent on the wreckage of whisky, in evoking a community in decline happy enough with handouts of the hard stuff.

After leaving Mackenzie, I went up to Milne's Bar, in Rose Street, to meet Norman MacCaig, a fastidious man with a purist approach to poetry and a corresponding fondness for malt whisky. 'Where have you been?' asked MacCaig between sips of Glen Grant, seeing I was more than usually pleased with myself. 'To see Compton Mackenzie.' Far from being impressed MacCaig snorted, 'Monty? He's an old bore.' MacCaig was wrong but I knew what he meant. Mackenzie, in the opinion of MacCaig (more a natural man in Assynt than Mackenzie's Ogilvie), was a commercially motivated writer who built his successful career on the easy option of ridiculing, thus exploiting, Scottish tradition. MacCaig saw a spiritual quality in Scotland, which is why he preferred malt to blended whisky, why he always stood on his dignity and avoided the obstreperous excesses of his fallen fellow boozers.

The contrast between Mackenzie and MacCaig is instructive: Scotland often seems to stagger between the extremes of blended whisky galore and malt in good measure. Scottish writers of this century have attempted, often obsessively, to understand to what extent the Scot has used, to what extent abused, his liquid assets.

Twentieth-century Scottish literature begins with a novel that has informed all the fiction that has followed. And George Douglas Brown's *The House with the Green Shutters* (1901) begins with a vision of a pub, the first sentence reading: 'The frowsy chambermaid of the Red Lion had just finished washing the front door steps.' For the psychodrama that unfolds in Brown's one and only novel, the Red Lion is as important as the eponymous House dominated by the domestic tyrant Old Gourlay, self-appointed monarch of all he surveys in Barbie. It is a home from home.

It is to the Red Lion that the maliciously gossiping 'bodies' of Barbie go for the 'matutinal dram'. It is to the Red Lion that Young Gourlay goes for the Scotch Courage he needs for a confrontation with his father. Having found 'that drink, to use his own language, gave him "smeddum"', Young Gourlay compensates for his cowardice by naming his own poison.

> With shaking knees Gourlay advanced to the bar, and, 'For God's sake, Aggie,' he whispered, 'give me a Kinblythmont!'

> It went at a gulp.
>
> 'Another!' he gasped, like a man dying of thirst, whom his first sip maddens for more. 'Another! Another!'

Suitably tanked up, Young Gourlay goes from the Red Lion to the Green Shutters and murders his father, smashing his head with a huge poker and causing him to fall on a fender. The fall of the House of Gourlay neatly symbolises the collapse of Scotland into a country conditioned to accept a caricature of itself. A country cursed by the hard stuff.

The whisky favoured by Young Gourlay is a blended whisky. Brown makes this quite clear in a conversation Young Gourlay has with Deacon Allardyce. Alluding to Young Gourlay's stint in Edinburgh as a student, the Deacon lisps, 'No doubt a man who knowth Edinburgh tho well as you, will have a favourite blend of his own.' 'I generally prefer Kinblythmont's Cure,' said Gourlay with the air of a connoisseur. 'But Anderson's Sting o' Delight's very good, and so's Balsillie's Brig o' the Mains.' Brown made Young Gourlay in the image of Scottish soaks to whom blended whisky is not so much a national drink as a national drug capable of changing gentle Jekyll into homicidal Hyde.

Stevenson, himself no stranger to drink, surely intended to simulate the impact of blended whisky on the constitution and imagination when, in *The Strange Case of Dr Jekyll and Mr Hyde* (1886), he allowed Dr Jekyll his first taste of the poison he never names. Inhibited by social conventions, the ingenious Jekyll blends his own drink. His description of the first mouthful could be confirmed by countless Scots scunnered by their first taste of the hard stuff that promises, and quickly brings, a murderous metamorphosis.

> I . . . drank off the potion [and] racking pangs succeeded: a grinding in the bones, deadly nausea, and a horror of the spirit that cannot be exceeded at the hour of birth or death. Then these agonies began swiftly to subside, and I came to myself as if out of a great sickness. There was something strange in my sensations, something indescribably new, and, from its very novelty, incredibly sweet. I felt younger, lighter, happier in body; within I was conscious of a heady recklessness, a current of disordered sensual images running like a mill-race in my fancy, a solution of the bonds of obligation, an unknown but not an innocent freedom of the soul.

A warped Faust, he has sold his soul to a demon drink and before long is capable of committing murder. A demon drink that alters the personality to a dangerous degree has to be soul-destroying.

So back to George Douglas Brown. A year after his extraordinary novel was published, T.W.H. Crosland brought out a vicious, therefore stimulating, polemic called *The Unspeakable Scot*, a title he thought Brown should have chosen for his chronicle of Barbie. As unmoved as Brown by the smugly sentimental fiction of the Kailyard novelists (Brown consciously composed his novel as an antidote to 'the sentimental slop of Barrie, and Crocket, and Maclaren') Crosland admired Brown's 'squalid picture' of life as lived in Scotland. After lambasting various Scots (including Burns), Crosland turned to what he perceived as the spirit of Scotland.

> Whiskey to breakfast, whiskey to dinner, whiskey to supper; whiskey when you meet a friend, whiskey over all business meetings whatsoever; whiskey before you go into the kirk, whiskey

> when you come out; whiskey when you are about to take a journey, whiskey all along the road, whiskey at journey's end; whiskey when you are well, whiskey if you be sick, whiskey almost as soon as you are born, whiskey the last thing before you die – that is Scotland . . . Whiskey, and that of the crudest and most shuddering quality, is undoubtedly the Scotchman's peculiar vanity. The amount that he can consume without turning a hair is quite appalling. I have seen a Scotchman drink three bottles of Glenlivet on a railway journey from King's Cross to Edinburgh, and when he got out at Edinburgh he strutted doucely to the refreshment bar and demanded further whiskey.

Carried away by his hyperbolic hatred, Crosland confuses crude soul-destroying whisky with smooth malts such as Glenlivet but the point is well made. In the eyes of the watching world, Scotland is synonymous with whisky. Why?

This question probably answers itself (the climate, the conditions, the culture) but prompts other, equally compelling, questions. Do Scottish writers like Brown relate blended whisky to spiritual ruin because they are reflecting reality? Or do they create an artistic image so enthralling that life in Scotland imitates art? Or is whisky itself, being more complex than Crosland is capable of understanding, not so much an indispensable part of the Scottish way of life and death as a phenomenon that requires closer scrutiny than any writer has so far attempted?

First things first. The psychological precedent Brown set in *Green Shutters* was regarded as a pattern to be copied by subsequent Scottish novelists, allowing them to arrange their experience in an increasingly familiar form.

J. MacDougall Hay's *Gillespie* (1914), which structurally and stylistically shadows *Green Shutters*, also opens with an image of an inn, appropriately named The Ghost since the book is full of Gothic horror. A man has been murdered in The Ghost and Alastair Campbell, who discovers the corpse, acts as a Scot is supposed to act: 'Campbell took to drink . . . Soon all the bottles in the bar were emptied.' Gillespie Strang, the Gourlay-like antihero of the novel, is born in the inn, and is killed by the whisky-curse that inhabits it, the bad spirit that haunts a house shaped as another symbol of Scotland.

Here's how. Towards the end of the novel Gillespie's alcoholic wife is 'seated at the fire, nursing a whisky bottle in her lap as it were a babe'. Hallucinating, she murders her son by slashing his throat with a razor then falls back and smashes her head on the back of a fender. Gillespie contracts lockjaw by stepping on one of his wife's broken whisky bottles and goes to The Ghost to die. At the end 'his lips were purple and stained with blood-froth'. Scotland, MacDougall Hay implies, is unable to escape from its deadly alcoholic inheritance.

Moving without comment past such unimaginative *Green Shutters* imitations as A.J. Cronin's first novel, *Hatter's Castle* (1931), we arrive at Lewis Grassic Gibbon's *Sunset Song* (1932), the first and finest book in the *Scots Quair* trilogy, which comes complete with a prelude containing an allusion to Brown's masterpiece: 'There wasn't a house with green shutters in the whole of Kinraddie.' Chris Guthrie, soulful daughter of the soil, has a dread of coarse creatures so marries Ewan Tavendale, a thoughtful working man. All goes well until Ewan, unable to endure the accusations of cowardice that cling to every pacifist in time of war, enlists in the army to do his bit in the First World War. When he comes home on leave, before going to fight in France, he is almost unrecognisable. Brutalised by army experience, he is transformed into a coarse creature so, of course, excessively fond of the hard stuff.

> Every day he went swaggering down the road and was off to Drumlithie, or Stonehaven or Fordoun, drinking there . . . Did she [Chris] think him still the young fool he had been, content to slave and slave at Blawearie – *without as much as a dram* to savour the soss . . . He'd made friends with Mutch, him that once he could hardly abide, and with him he went drinking each night on their drunken sprees.

Ewan has turned into a domestic tyrant in the Gourlay tradition; Chris saves herself from a wife-battering only by defending herself with a kitchen knife. Again, the spiritual fall of the Scot is indicated by a progressive – that is, regressive – reliance on the hard stuff.

One of the most violent of Scottish novels, and that's saying something, is the Glasgow slumland saga *No Mean City* (1935) by H. Kingsley Long and Alexander McArthur: so vividly did it fix the Gorbals in the public mind as an inferno unfit for human habitation that a recent approach to Glasgow City Council to mount a plaque in memory of McArthur, who committed suicide in 1947, was turned down on the grounds that 'McArthur did neither Glasgow nor the Gorbals any favours by writing his book'. Johnnie Stark rules the Gorbals of the 1920s as the 'Razor King', slashing the faces of his foes with relish. An archetypal hardman, he graduates from gratuitous violence to organised crime when he masterminds a whisky raid on a pub.

After the raid there is a celebration in Johnnie's single end.

> Thirty young people, men and girls, assembled in that single apartment and settled down to the solemnly deliberate business of drinking whisky until they could drink no more . . . But Johnnie missed only one day from his work. His iron constitution enabled him to throw off the effects of alcohol much sooner than most men [so] he would be back for more whisky in the evening, fit and fresh and dangerous.

Johnnie loses his battle with the bottle, knocking back like Jekyll first tasting the potion: 'Johnnie found that the first swallow of whisky made him feel sick again, but another gulp steadied him and put fresh heart into him.' Before his last battle the hardman has his last fling.

> The raw whisky was a fire in his parched throat . . . What he had drunk would not have been enough to have the slightest effect on him in the old days. Now he was exhilarated and did not realise the cause.

He walks into another fight and is kicked to death. Unfortunately, the scenario is all too plausible, enabling us to answer the question of whether the mainstream Scottish novel reflects the reality of an abuse of the hard stuff. Undoubtedly it does, which does not mean we are forever bound to live and die by that reality. Answering another question, we need not imitate the art of the mainstream Scottish novel.

If the mainstream Scottish novel is hardened by the hard stuff, genres are scarcely less so, always associating the hard stuff with the recklessly rough Scot. *Five Red Herrings* (1931), the thriller honorary Scot Dorothy L. Sayers set in Kirkcudbright and Gatehouse of Fleet, offers a portrait of the artist as a Scot, a man regularly made riotous by whisky: 'Campbell, the landscape painter, had had maybe one or two more wee ones than was absolutely necessary, especially for a man with red hair, and their effect had been to make him even more militantly Scottish than usual.' The combative Campbell is murdered, to the delight of those who had to endure his verbal violence, and it is left to gentleman detective Lord Peter Wimsey to solve the mystery.

William McIlvanney's ungentlemanly detective, Inspector Jack Laidlaw, is a hardman who deals out rough justice to violent criminals, flashing his fists with the worst of them. He is, of course, a whisky drinker: 'I take water with my whisky,' Laidlaw said. 'Not condescension.' That Chandleresque quip, from *The Papers of Tony Veitch* (1983), is typical of a man deeply versed in the alcoholic culture of the Scottish cities where hardmen 'dispensed a pure and undiluted product – 100 per cent proof violence'. At the end of *Tony Veitch*, Laidlaw drinks his way from pub to pub in Glasgow then, waiting for a taxi, sees a sight that prompts one of the best jokes in Scottish fiction about the whisky-drinker. Seeing a man playing a mouth-organ for money, Laidlaw feels generous.

> Reaching into his pocket to reward impertinence, Laidlaw took out a handful of coins, selected a couple and remarked philosophically to Gus, 'Notice that, when you're on the batter? Finish up with pockets like a street-bookie. See, you always buy more with notes. Coins are beneath you. You become a whisky millionaire.'

Scotland is full of whisky millionaires, an ironic comment on a country that is rich in resources – including whisky – it squanders.

Looking for an alternative tradition to the violence of

the hard stuff is an unsatisfying quest. The only Scottish novelist of stature to state seriously the case for malt whisky was Neil Gunn, who had considerable expertise on the subject, serving from 1923 to 1937 as Excise Officer attached to the Glen Mhor distillery in Inverness (we have it on David Daiches' authority, in his *Scotch Whisky* of 1969, that 'Glen Mhor is one of the truly great post-prandial whiskies, full, rich and mellow'). Disappointingly, Gunn does not inform his novels with his professional expertise, his characters knocking back whisky indiscriminately. Admittedly, Kenn, the autobiographical hero of *Highland River* (1937), is given 'an unopened bottle of Black and White' but elsewhere the whisky is anonymous: in *The Well at the World's End* (1951), 'when Lachlan got his tumbler he looked at the largeness of the whisky inside it': in *The Other Landscape* (1954), 'The Major poured a gush of whisky into a tumbler . . . and Lachlan swallowed the dram in one swoop.'

It is not the fiction but the discursive *Whisky and Scotland* (1935), that contains Gunn's spiritual credo and an excessively romantic thing it is, sometimes as sentimental as the Kailyardism that Gunn defends ('the Kailyard . . . carried over in its fashion the love of learning'). Gunn argues that malt whisky is the magical distillation of the Celtic people, and he looks back longingly to 'the Golden Age' when men were Gaels and whisky was sweet to the Gael-speaking tongue, 'purer than any water from any well'. Appalled by the caricature of the Scot sozzled on the hard stuff, Gunn creates an equally unacceptable caricature – of the gentle Gael inspired by 'a good cause and a noble drink'.

It is irresponsible to imply that there was a golden age of unfailingly exquisite malt whisky that was destroyed by the successive blows of the Excise Act of 1823, Aeneas

Coffey's patent still of 1830, the formation of DCL in 1877. Burns, an exciseman like Gunn and the poet most memorably associated with whisky, wrote in a letter of 22 December 1788: 'The Whisky of this country [meaning Dumfriesshire in particular, not Scotland in general] is a most rascally liquor; and by consequence, only drunk by the most rascally part of the inhabitants.' Still, Burns remains the most able exponent of the joys of whisky and is one of the first (for Fergusson came before) to establish that poets, not novelists, are the most lucid commentators on whisky, as we shall see.

Meanwhile, it is worth noting that malt whisky is hardly savoured in recent Scottish fiction, judging by the products of the self-appointed Great Glasgow Novelists. For the professional Glaswegian, self-consciously a common man of the people, the malt whisky man is a smoothie or a sentimentalist, usually both. Alasdair Gray's *Lanark* (1981), confronts the interchangeable artistic imaginations of writer Lanark and painter Duncan Thaw with the matter of Scotland. When Lanark meets a smoothie in a mansion, the smoothie is predictably a man for malt whisky.

> He was nearly seven feet high and wore a polo-necked sweater and well-cut khaki trousers and, though perhaps fifty, gave an impression of youthful fitness . . . He turned to a sideboard with bottles and glasses on it [and asked Lanark what he would like to drink].
>
> 'Nothing.'
>
> 'Nothing. Well, sit down anyway. I want you to tell me something. Meanwhile I will pour myself [some] Glenlivet Malt. Here's health.'

It is soon apparent to Lanark that, for all his smooth talk

and smooth manner and smooth malt whisky, 'the tall man was drunk' and talking nonsense even if elegant nonsense, unlike the prole in the pub with his raw blended whisky and supposedly sound common sense (pull the other one, it's got Bell's).

Gray's *1982 Janine* (1984), in which the narrator meditates on sex and Scotland while doing his solitary drinking in a hotel room, is specifically cited as the vision of an alcoholic: 'I am certainly alcoholic, but not a drunkard.' His opinion of Glasgow is of a city perpetually hungover by the past: 'Glasgow now means nothing to the rest of Britain but unemployment, drunkenness and out-of-date radical militancy.' His own hope of escape is to step out of the stereotype that traps all Glaswegians, which means finding an alternative to the hard stuff: 'Lie on a beach under a warm sun. Drink wine, not spirits.' Wine, not malt whisky, please note, is equated with civilised drinking.

James Kelman's *A Disaffection* (1989), about a frustrated Glasgow schoolteacher who dreams of doing something creative ('his secret hankering was to be a painter, doing fairly large murals') as one way out of the urban nightmare, simulates the linguistic register of the free-swearing proletariat so there is much fucking about in the book. Kelman's vision of the proletarian Eden is satirical, a matter of having enough money to acquire sensual comforts including a supply of malt whisky.

> The Glaswegian male doesn't ask much in this man's army, just an umbrella and the occasional fish supper, a nice looking woman and big win on the fucking football pools. Then one could fuck off to a pleasant cosy wee hotel in the Inner Hebrides, there to partake of single-malt goldies in the company of one's partner, thence off

> upstairs to a large double bed with views of the boisterous Atlantic, waves thrashing the shore . . .

Glaswegians, of course, fancy themselves as lapsed Gaels and this dream of a spiritual homecoming to the promised land is made nightmarish by the realisation that the promised land is now inhabited by tourists, including Glaswegians on the batter.

Our last look at modern Scottish literature must give due credit to Hugh MacDiarmid, whose *A Drunk Man Looks at the Thistle* (1926), in my view the greatest literary work produced in Scotland in the 20th century, opens with an onslaught on the hard stuff that passes as whisky in Scotland. MacDiarmid, a connoisseur of malt whisky, knew what he was talking about when he put the following lines in the mouth of his immortal Drunk Man:

> Forbye, the stuffie's no' the real Mackay,
> The sun's sel' aince, as sune as ye began it,
> Riz in your vera saul: but what keeks in
> Noo is in truth the vilest 'saxpenny planet'.
>
> And as the worth's gane doun the cost has risen,
> Yin canna throw the cockles o' yin's hert
> Wi' oot ha'en' cauld feet noo, jalousin' what
> The wife'll say (I dinna blame her fur't).
>
> It's robbin Peter to pey Paul at least . . .
> And a' that's Scotch aboot it is the name,
> Like a' thing else ca'd Scottish nooadays
> – A' destitute o' speerit juist the same.

A Drunk Man is an alcoholic odyssey that takes a typical Scot, initially as much a caricature of the genuine article as blended whisky is of malt whisky ('The sun's sel' aince'), and transforms him into an inviolable individual inspired by spirituality rather than the spirit of the hard stuff.

Little wonder that MacCaig, who drank glass for glass of malt with the master, chose to address MacDiarmid (born Christopher Murray Grieve) in the Envoi of his 'Ballade of Good Whisky', from *Collected Poems* (1962).

> Chris! (whether perpendicular or flat
> Or moving rather horribly aslant)
> Here is a toast that you won't scunner at –
> Glenfiddich, Bruichladdich and Glengrant!

MacCaig paid attention to the Drunk Man's advice 'To be yersel's – and to mak' that worth bein"; though he was the occasionally drunk man MacDiarmid valued most in Scotland in his later years, MacCaig never made the mistake of attempting to flatter his celebrated friend through imitation. MacCaig never wrote in Scots, synthetic or otherwise, and his pointedly short metaphysical poems in English are light years away, in technique and tone, from MacDiarmid's unfinished epic 'Cornish Heroic Song' in celebration of the Celtic consciousness.

Unfortunately, MacDiarmid's disciples lacked the alcoholic taste of the master. Sydney Goodsir Smith, one of the most convivial characters to set up a series of second homes in Rose Street – Edinburgh's amber mile of pubs – was an indiscriminate drinker who could knock back almost anything that contained an alcoholic kick. When he wrote about whisky he named his blend, as in 'Song: The Steeple Bar, Perth':

> O it's dowf tae be drinkin' alane, my luve,
> When I wud drink wi my dear,
> Nor Crabbie nor Bell's can fire me, luve,
> As they wud an you were here.

Smith's volume *The Wanderer* (1943), contains his best-known lyric, 'Ma Moujik Lass', which dwells on the theme of the solitary drinker:

> O fain I'd loo ma moujik lass,
> O fain I'd haud her breist –
> I've nocht tae haud but a whisky glass,
> A gey wanchancy feast.

Here the hard stuff is neither a cup of cheer nor a vessel for violence but a cup to cry into; the lyric accurately indicates the self-pitying sentimentality of the Scot who drowns his sorrows in drink.

MacDiarmid, the least sentimental of Scottish writers, was never a solitary drinker and, for all his trials and tribulations, never felt sorry for himself. The last time I saw MacDiarmid, shortly before he died of cancer in 1978, his love of malt whisky was undiminished. I went out to his home in Biggar with Harry Stamper, the actor whose one-man play, *Between the Wars*, is an uncanny impersonation of the poet. As both Harry and I lived at the time in Markinch, 'the home of Haig's', we brought MacDiarmid a half bottle of Haig's as a present. He wouldn't touch it. 'Leave it somewhere,' he chuckled, 'and bring over that lemonade there.' That 'lemonade' turned out to be a bottle of Glenmorangie. MacDiarmid drank several glasses with relish as he reminisced about his long life as a poet and stirrer-up of Scotland. He assured us that malt whisky was what had kept him alive for so long and we left when the bottle was empty, feeling full of the real Scottish spirit.

Yes, whisky requires closer scrutiny than any writer has so far attempted. MacDiarmid's Drunk Man laid low the masculine myth of the hard stuff, but left malt whisky alone. Thus malt whisky is a muse that still awaits its true creative coming.

You whose ambition is to swim the Minch
Or write a drum concerto in B flat
Or run like Bannister or box like Lynch
Or find the Ark wrecked on Mt Ararat –
No special training's needed: thin or fat,
You'll do it if you never once supplant
As basis of your commissariat
Glenfiddich, Bruichladdich and Glengrant.

My own desires are small. In fact, I flinch
From heaving a heavenly Hindu from her ghat
Or hauling Loch Ness monsters, inch by inch,
Out of their wild and watery habitat.
I've no desire to be Jehoshaphat

Or toy with houris fetched from the Levant.
But give to me – *bis dat qui cito dat* –
Glenfiddich, Bruichladdich and Glengrant.

I would drink down, and think the feat a cinch,
The Congo, Volga, Amazon, La Platte,
And Tweed as chaser – a bargain, this, to clinch
In spite of *nota bene* and *caveat*
(Though what a feast must follow after that
Of Amplex, the divine deodorant!) –
If they ran – hear my heart go pit-a-pat! –
Glenfiddich, Bruichladdich and Glengrant.

Envoi
Chris! (whether perpendicular or flat
Or moving rather horribly aslant)
Here is a toast that you won't scunner at –
Glenfiddich, Bruichladdich and Glengrant!

[*Editor's Note*: Hugh MacDiarmid's poetry and writings had a profound effect on many Scots during his lifetime. This essay, written in 1952, encapsulates his attitude to drinking and to Scotch whisky. It was published in a book entitled *The Uncanny Scot* in 1968.]

GLASGOW! 'This savage, wild, ridiculous city', as the playwright 'James Bridie' called it, in a speech in which he very properly praised 'the right kind of lunatic, daft, Scottish panache', an attribute most easily encountered in the pubs, but difficult to find elsewhere except (by accident) in the course of a battle, a political meeting, a love affair, a theological wrangle, or a literary controversy.

I have never been able, despite repeated efforts, to understand the periodicity of those complaints against the Scottish pub which have been made during the past half century. Made, I suspect, when not by women or clergymen, either by English visitors or by Scots who, as Sir Walter Scott said, 'unScotched make damned bad Englishmen'. They are usually accompanied by envious comparisons with the amenities of English inns, which we are told are far more sociable and cater to family parties in a way Scottish pubs do not. For, in the latter, at their most typical, the rule is 'men only' and 'no sitting' – you stand at the counter with your toes in that narrow sawdust-filled trough which serves as a comprehensive combined ashtray, litter-bin and cuspidor. So it was when I first began to drink nearly 50 years ago; so it still is for the most part. Certainly nowadays, in addition to the common bars and to the jug (or family) departments to which women, mostly of a shawled, slatternly and extremely subfusc order, still repair with all the ancient furtiveness, there are bright chromium-fitted saloon bars, cocktail bars and other modern accessories in the more pretentious places. And even in most of the ordinary bars there is now a fair sprinkling of women not only of the 'lower orders' or elderly at that, but gay young things, merry widows, and courtesans. Men (if you can call them that) even take their wives and daughters along with them to these meretricious deScotticised resorts.

Now, I am not a misogynist by any means. I simply believe there is a time and a place for everything – yes, literally, everything. And like a high proportion of my country's regular and purposive drinkers I greatly prefer a complete absence of women on occasions of libation. I also prefer a complete absence of music and very little illumination. I am therefore a strong supporter of the lower – or lowest – type of 'dive' where drinking is the principal purpose and no one wants to be distracted from that absorbing business by music, women, glaring lights, chromium fittings, too many mirrors unless sufficiently fly-spotted and mildewed, or least of all, any fiddling trivialities of *l'art nouveau*. If there are still plenty of pubs in Glasgow which conform to these requirements and remain frowsy and fusty enough to suit my taste and that of my boon companions, in another respect the old order has changed sadly and I fear irreversibly. Our Scottish climate – not to speak of the soot-laden, catarrh-producing atmosphere of Glasgow in particular – makes us traditionally great spirit-drinkers. That has changed. Most of us cannot afford – or at any rate cannot get – much whisky or, for that matter, any other spirit. There are, of course, desperate characters who drink methylated spirits. I have known – and still know – resolute souls partial to a mixture of boot-blacking and 'meth', and I remember when I was in the Merchant Service during the recent war a few hardy characters who went to the trouble of stealing old compasses off the boats at Greenock (where we had the largest small-boat pool in Europe) in order to extract from them the few drops of spirit (well mixed with crude-oil and verdigris) they contained. But in Glasgow pubs today at least 90 per cent of the drinking is of beer – and mere 'swipes' at that; 'beer' that never saw a hop. I can remember the time when it was the other way about. What beer was consumed was used simply as a 'chaser' to the whisky in precisely the same way as a 'boilermaker' in New York. For of course you get drunk quicker on whisky plus water than on neat whisky, and whisky and soda is an English monstrosity no true Scot can countenance at all.

There are other sorry changes in even the lowest-down pubs which in general hold to the grim old tradition of the true Scottish 'boozer'. The question of hours, for example. In London one can still drink legally 23 hours out of 24. That is because London is a congeries of different boroughs which have different 'permitted hours' so that by switching from one borough at closing time it is easy to find another where 'they' will still be open for an hour or two longer. In Glasgow, moreover, unlike London, there are few facilities for drinking outside the permitted hours. For most people, that is. It will hardly be thought that I am pleading for decreased consumption, but I believe that the same amount of strong drink taken in a leisurely way over a fair number of hours is less harmful than the rush to squeeze in the desired number of drinks in the short time the law allows. Our national poet, Robert Burns, was right when he said: 'Freedom and whisky gang thegither.' What he meant is precisely what my own motto means: 'They do not love liberty who fear licence.' I speak for that large body of my compatriots who uphold this great principle and regard respectability and affectation of any kind a sour deadliest enemy. There are, of course, clubs and hotels, but *hoi polloi* have nothing to do with either of these.

Only a few years ago there were also Burns Clubs which took advantage of a loophole in the law and did a roaring trade especially on Sundays. You did not require to be introduced. You simply paid half-a-crown at the door and automatically became a member for the day. The difficulty – especially for the thirsty stranger within the gates, and indeed for the bulk of the citizens themselves – was to find these places. One heard about them. One heard, indeed, fantastic tales of the alcoholic excesses which went on there. But they were exceedingly difficult to find. You had to be 'in the know'. Suddenly they disappeared entirely. I have never been able to discover why. There was nothing in the press – and I could learn nothing over my private grapevine either – about police action having been taken. They must have been very profitable to those who ran them, and a substantial source of revenue to the 'liquor trade' generally. They served a very useful purpose since no one not resident in a hotel and not a member of a club could otherwise get a drink in Glasgow on Sundays. (It was – and is still – jolly difficult to get a meal even.)

During these two wars there were all kinds of interferences with the incidence and duration of the 'permitted hours'. Quite a proportion of licence-holders got it into their heads that they could close earlier than the decreed closing time – and even take a weekly half-holiday and in some cases shut shop and go off for a week's holiday in the summer time. They still do, and act arbitrarily in many other ways. All that is, of course, quite illegal, although the magistracy and police authorities turned a blind eye at these irregularities and even welcomed them. The fact is, of course, as the very term 'public house' shows, that the condition of the licence obliges the licence-holder to have his place at the disposal of citizens at all times – not necessarily for drinking at all; a citizen is entitled to have the use of these places whenever he wants if only to use the lavatory or shelter from the weather, or read his newspaper, or meet a friend. It would, in practice, be virtually impossible to fight this and other corrupt practices the authorities have winked at. Recognising this, some of us tried to organise a 'Consumers' Union', since the consumers are the only unorganised and helpless factor in the liquor situation. It proved impossible; the consumers won't combine. They are far too individualistic. Though such a Consumers' Union might have been very useful in certain connections *vis-à-vis* the Liquor Trade, the Municipal, State and Police Authorities and every variety of blue-nosed snooper, I am on many other counts enough of an 'unregenerate sinner' not to regret that the effort failed. Yet at times I like to toy with the idea that if it had been possible to organise even a high proportion of pub-users (leaving out consumers who consume elsewhere) the result would have been one of the strongest organisations in the world. No Trade Union, or combination of Trade Unions, would have been a patch on it.

I trust I have made myself clear. The majority of Glasgow pubs are for connoisseurs of the morose, for those who relish the element of degradation in all boozing and do not wish to have it eliminated by the introduction of music, modernistic fitments, arty effects, or other extraneous devices whatsoever. It is the old story of those who prefer hard-centre chocolates to soft, storm to sunshine, sour to sweet. True Scots always prefer the former of these opposites That is one of our principal differences from the English. We do not like the confiding, the intimate, the ingratiating, the hail-fellow-well-met, but prefer the unapproachable, the hard-bitten, the recalcitrant, the sinister, the malignant, the sarcastic, the saturnine, the cross-grained and the cankered, and the howling wilderness to the amenities of civilisation, the irascible to the affable, the prickly to the smooth. We have no damned fellow-feeling at all, and look at ourselves and others with the eye of a Toulouse Lautrec appraising an obscene old toe-rag doing the double split. In short, we are all poets (all true Scots – that is, all Scots not encased in a carapace of conventionality a mile thick) of *l'humour noir* and, as William Blake said, 'All poets are of the devil's party'.

There is a well-known story about Carlyle and Emerson spending several hours together without exchanging a word. Carlyle declared it was one of the best nights he ever spent with anybody. A lot of us spend many nights in Scottish pubs in the same way and we agree with

Carlyle. Scotland produces a type of man who can dispense more completely than any with what James Joyce called 'the atrocities of human intercourse'.

There is nothing less exportable than a national sense of humour. The Scottish temper I am writing about is little known abroad. Our internationally famous comedians purvey a very different account of us. The sorry joke is that so many Scots believe the latter and model themselves all too successfully on it. Yet what I am trying to express is well-enough known about us in other connections. It is this that for centuries has made the Scottish soldier famous as a bayonet-fighter. A similar preference for naked steel runs through every phase of our life. It is summed up in the old Gaelic proverb: 'Fingal's sword never needs to cut twice.' Burns says in one of his poems that you need not be 'nice' with him. The only kind of friendships one makes – or wishes to make or could tolerate at all – in such pubs was well described by my Irish friend, the late W.B. Yeats, when he wrote:

> I called him a knave and a fool –
> But friendship never dies!

In other words, the injunction which is as one with the very marrow of our bones is 'Woe to him of whom all men speak well.' We have no use for emotions, let alone sentiments, but are solely concerned with passions.

One of the best essayists on aspects of Scottish literature, Mr J.D. Scott, has pointed out how deep in Scottish life are the roots of this 'slow and vicious enjoyment', this 'formidable and ferocious scorn'. It is the tremendous animating principle of three of the greatest modern Scottish novels – George Douglas Brown's *House with the Green Shutters*, R.L. Stevenson's unfinished *Weir of Hermiston* and Sydney Goodsir Smith's super-Rabelaisian story of Edinburgh today (doing for it what Joyce's *Ulysses* did for Dublin), *Carotid Cornucopius*. It is precisely this element, utterly different from English humour, that is the essence of any number of the most typical Scottish anecdotes. Like, for example, the story of the minister who told his congregation that in a dream he had seen them all in Hell suffering the tortures of the damned. 'Ye lifted up your eyes to the Almighty God and ye said to Him, "O Lord, we didna ken it would be like this," and the Lord Almighty (*slowly and unctuously*), in His infinite mercy and compassion, looked down upon ye and He said, "Well, noo ye ken!"'

We (if I may speak for all of us) do not go to pubs for chit-chat, we do not wish them crossed with some sort of café or tea-party or concert or damned *conversazione*; we are fond enough of our womenfolk, but there are times when we want away from them as no doubt there are times when they want to be away from us. The keynote of Glasgow life is still expressed in the song sung by Will Fyffe, the great Scottish comedian, which runs:

> I belong to Glasgow,
> Dear old Glasgow toon.
> But what's the matter wi' Glasgow?
> For it's going roon' and roon'.
> I'm only a common old working chap,
> As anyone here can see,
> But when I get a couple o' drinks on a Saturday,
> Glasgow belongs to me.

Our attitude is not inhuman. We are experienced men of the world. We like what we like to be a little grim – in keeping with the facts of life, and loathe facile emotions. We cherish no illusions, and consequently prefer a mutual taciturnity to any sort of social joy, standing shoulder to shoulder with other men we do not know from Adam and do not want to know. We feel no necessity whatsoever to indulge in any airs and graces, are not fond of promiscuous conversation, at least of any sustained sort, and if our risible faculties are moved at all by the human spectacle, that movement only adorns our faces intermittently with some sort of *risus sardonicus* that in flickering across our features barely interrupts the emission of the dense smoke of the black tobacco going well in our clay pipes. It is, indeed, a sort of fleeting facial comment hardly distinguishable from the effect of that gagging which an unwarily deep swig at what passes for Scotch whisky is apt to etch on the granitic features of even the most hardened soak.

Elsewhere I have summed up my regard for Glasgow in a brief poem, 'Placenta Previa', which runs:

> It'll be no easy matter to keep the dirt in its place
> And get the Future out alive in *this* case.

On the last Hogmanay night (New Year's Eve), as on all its predecessors, no matter how dourly and darkly I take my pleasures, the same way some people keep snakes for pets, I once again, with a great upsurge of savage joy, recalled another verse of mine and practised what I preached, namely:

> O this is the time for all mankind
> To rejoice without a doubt
> – And break the neck of the bottle
> If the cork will not come out!

And that is precisely how Scots do bring in the New Year. They gather in the public squares of their cities and towns, and as the bells ring out the Old Year and ring in the New, they empty their bottles and smash them on the street. On this most recent Hogmanay I was one of a company of many uproarious hundreds doing this in George Square, Glasgow, undeterred by the fact that a day of gale and sleet was given way to snow and ice and that hundreds of people in Glasgow alone had been rendered homeless by blown-down houses or injured in the streets by falling chimney-pots and torn-off slates.

A wild night, so our merriment had to be correspondingly wild to lift our hearts above its hazards. A typical incident was the ripping apart of a newly built school. It was hurled by the gale towards a house occupied by a family of Kellys. One section of the steel-framed school was lifted in the air and wrapped round an electric standard at the Kellys' back fence. That standard saved the Kelly house. If it hadn't been there the school would have gone right through the house.

Hail Caledonia, stern and wild!

Scott Fitzgerald speaks of 'Jay Gatsby breaking up like glass against Tom Buchanan's hard malice'. I sometimes think all the shams and unveracities in the world will break up in the same way against the Scottish spirit of which I am writing. Scots of that particular mettle are the very salt of the earth. I am one of them and so I know. It would not pay anyone to dispute the point in any of the Glasgow pubs I frequent.

Let me finish this Scottish letter on a different note altogether. Otherwise it will not be true to Scotland, which is a country of sharp transitions and extraordinary variety, in its landscape, weather, people and everything else. Glasgow is only a part of it, and utterly unrepresentative of the rest. Well, I was talking to an Edinburgh man yesterday and I said something about the inexplicable character of Scottish scenery, and Scottish life. And he pulled me up at once. 'Nonsense,' he said, 'there is nothing inexplicable – nothing to account for which almost anybody cannot devise at once some reasonable hypothesis.' And he challenged me to give an example. I replied that I was walking across a moor in Ross-shire one summer afternoon. There wasn't a soul in sight, hardly an animal, only a bird or two. It was almost 12 miles to the nearest village. Suddenly among the heather I spied a yellow glove. It was almost brand-new, did not look as if it had been worn at all. I picked it up and as I did so I heard a clicking noise inside it. I took it by the tip of one of the fingers and shook it gently – and out fell four fingernails and a thumbnail, the complete set of nails from one hand. They were perfectly clean, like seashells. However they had come off it had quite obviously neither been through disease nor violence. It was impossible to conceive a man drawing off his glove and his nails with it, tossing them into the heather, and walking on unaware, or, if aware, as if nothing had happened. I found it – and find it – impossible to imagine the state of mind of a man who a few miles further on discovered he had done just that. I have been haunted ever since by a sense of the horrible blunt feeling of nailless fingertips. I should have thought in such a case a man would have reported the matter to the police or discussed it with friends and that somehow or other news of such an extraordinary occurrence would have got round and out, and even into the papers. I made all sorts of enquiries and found that nothing was known or could be discovered about the matter. I enquired of medical friends and found that no known disease could account for it and that no similar case was cited in any medical or scientific book known to them.

I have never succeeded in solving the mystery or getting any light on it at all. But it can certainly serve as a parable of much that has happened in what has been called 'the self-suppression of the Scot' and the way he has sloughed off his literature, history, native languages and much else in the past two and a half centuries. Another and equal mystery is the way in which he is today resuming them, just as if the nailless finger-ends were suddenly growing new nails. There is widespread agreement that a great Scottish National Reawakening is in progress. I'd know more about that if I could hit on any explanation of the preceding loss. As matters stand, I take it, in the Scots law phrase, to *avizandum*, i.e. defer for further consideration. And yet I am conscious of my inability to make up my mind to deal with the situation because there are no facts on which one *can* make up one's mind, and a pressing desire to seize on small clues, to build up something in order that one may do something – *anything* – knowing all the time that if one *did* do something it would probably be wrong because the basic facts are missing. Whether I am right or not in fancying that this is something that could only have happened in Scotland, I think it will be agreed that it is exceedingly unlikely ever to have happened anywhere before and highly improbably that it will ever happen again. Above all, I wonder how the hell I invented it at all. Apart from just being Scotch, of course – really Scotch.

[Editor's Note: In March 1972 the poet, song-writer and novelist Stuart McGregor – author of *The Sinner* and *The Myrtle and Ivy* – left for Jamaica, where he was to take up a temporary medical post. As a student at Edinburgh University in the 1950s Stuart had been a vital driving force in the early days of the Scottish Folk Revival, and was the effective founder of the Edinburgh University Folk Song Society; one of his songs (*'Sandy Bell's Man'*) is still popular. He was tragically killed in a car crash less than a year after arriving in Jamaica. The song is, of course, to the tune of *'The Silver Tassie'*.]

Gae fetch tae us twa bolls o' malt,
The best that Sandy's can provide us,
And syne anither twa lay doon
As sure's we get the first inside us.
Scotch drink and sang hae aye been fieres;
Whisky and Stuart gang thegither:
Saw when the partin' gless we've drained,
We'll no be sweir tae hae anither!

The boat that rocks beside the pier
Will rock some mair when ye are on it.
Its deck will tilt and stand up hie
Tae match the tilt o' Stuart's bonnet.
On Kingston strand the dusky dames
For sportive romps will soon prepare 'em;
Spyin' the shape o' things to come,
They'll soon resolve tae grin an' bear 'em.

Stuart, atween us braid maun roll
'A waste of seas' – a vale o' water,
(What signifies a waste o' seas?
A waste o' beer's anither maitter.)
But in their cups, in auld Bell's Bar,
The legion o' the damned will mind ye,
And howp that, noo and then, ye'll toast
The gallus crew ye've left behind ye.

First, a poem:

We are sitting tonight in the fireglow, just you and I alone.
And the flickering light falls softly on a beauty that's all your own,
It glawms where your round smooth shoulder, from a graceful neck sweeps down;
And I would not exchange your beauty for the best dressed belle in town.

I have drawn the curtain closer, and from my easy chair,

I stretch my hands towards you, just to feel that
you are there.
And your breath is laden with perfume, and my
thoughts around you twine,
And I feel my pulses breathing as your spirit is
mingled with mine.

When the woes of the world have vanished,
When I've pressed my lips to yours; and to feel
your life blood flowing
To me is the best of cures . . .

And so in lyrical vein, continues this dewy-eyed tribute to a bottle of Sandy MacNab's Old Blended, since Scotch can inspire a depth of devotion in the breasts of certain Scotsmen which is not necessarily reproduced were they to stumble to tongue-tied explanation of the affection they feel for their lawfully wedded wives.

The drinking of whisky has, after all, given birth to many social rituals which are peculiarly masculine, and in which women may play only the most peripheral of roles.

Women in contemporary society do of course drink whisky. In fact, it must probably be admitted that those who do are prone to resorting to an array of mixers which do little to celebrate the blenders' art. But what they do not do, in the general run of these matters, is enter bars on their own and order a succession of whiskies washed down with half pints of warm beer, a combination as popular as it is lethal. They go out drinking in groups, but they tend not to go out in groups specifically to drink. They do not equate social standing with capacity, and whilst they may sympathise with a companion who becomes demonstrably the waur o' wear, they neither revere nor boast of her exploits.

It may come as profound shock to certain groups of men that women are remarkably underwhelmed by their supposed attractions when they are in the advanced state of whisky fever. One of the great unpublished truisms is that the more men drink the more irresistible they suppose themselves to become and the more determined are their female targets to offer maximum resistance. Drunk men fall into two broad categories, the aggressive and the pretty silly – the first are unbearable, the second are unbeddable, and neither can be taken home to mother.

But it is not just historical accident or precedent which made the male of the Scots species into an exclusively one-gender, secretive society. The track record of the distillers in marketing and advertising their liquid gold is a powerful reinforcement of social conditioning.

Since we must suppose that distillers, in common with all other segments of the retail segment centre, have a desire to maximise profitability, it is more than passing strange that they have traditionally behaved as if 52 per cent of the population failed to exist. Or, to be accurate, failed to drink the water of life.

Let us take a brief sojourn through some of the most popular whisky advertisements which have graced the full colour pages of magazines and newspapers. A very small percentage of them will be seen to feature women at all. More popularly they will feature soldiers, sportsmen, airmen or seamen; much clan chiefery, many supposed captains of industrial regiments. The message is clear and far from subliminal; real men may not eat quiche, but they have minimal difficulty disposing of the drams. Be a man and drink up. (Be a man and fall down.)

Where women are permitted to stray into this gallant celebration of the masculine virtues, their roles are quite clearly defined. A remarkable number of popular adverts feature Mr Sauve in a variety of sartorially elegant guises with a well-turned glass at his hand and a bottle of refills at his elbow on a tray. With him, here clinging shyly to the crook of his manly arm, there leaning expectantly over the dinner table, now at his feet as he convalesces, then gazing in mute admiration at his conversational flow, are a succession of props. Female props. Women whose unstated but emphatic function is to be seen rather than heard, to serve as helpmeet, audience, factotum, fiancée, nursemaid and groupie. Incredibly none of them has been permitted a glass of her own, though one, daringly and inexpertly, grasps a cigarette.

There may of course be some subtlety in the marketing strategy which has totally failed to impinge on my profoundly uncommercial consciousness. But why do you imagine all of these women are supposed not to indulge at all? It can't be because they are not regarded as consumers and purchasers. After all, another raft of these ads shows the little woman either agonising over what to give her Lord and Master as a token of festive affection (answer: a case of whisky), or what to put down against the names of problem male relatives and friends on her Christmas shopping list (answer: a bottle of whisky). Yet while she is seen as having purchasing power at one remove, she is never depicted as a beneficiary of the much lauded and all embracing benefit of *uisge beatha* in her own right.

And, to a large extent, that is still true of sales techniques today. The revolution which has overtaken drinking habits in the last quarter of this century has included the ready availability of alcohol within the supermarket and grocery premises. Here we have an opportunity for the salesman to pitch his tent and perfect his pitch right in the heart of what is still, regrettably, largely a female domain. But are they out there demanding that we eschew G&T in favour of the clean-cut pleasures of our own home brew; have they devised new television strategies making it clear that today's up and at 'em female exec carries only a credit card, Filofax and – strictly for emergencies – handbag flask?

Not at all. They have, of course, acknowledged that women are now a part of the pub culture. The drinks industry had even, golly gosh, felt able to allow all-women groups to drink beer whilst gently sending up the fanciable waiter. But they have majored on selling to women the notion that what their girlish hearts most desire is a series of over-priced, allegedly exotic liqueur-style potions. They come in sensually shaped bottles with elegant labels and are sold as the basis for a series of suggestive cocktails. Nobody has failed to spot the obvious join between social drinking and sexuality, but nobody, it seems, thinks that women and whisky have very much to do with the equation. So the smarter bars offer a series of concoctions with insinuating names, guaranteed to make the young female client wide-eyed and, very probably, legless.

Some customers, however, underline the female capacity for steadfastness in the face of terrible visual odds. There have been, over the years, very many experiments on the impact of colour on appetite. How then can it be that women can be sold, and will drink, liquid inventions of electric hues, or tip into liqueurs mixers which give the resultant offering all the obvious appeal of the average potion for bowel disorders? Why, in short, is it supposed that women will fall upon high-priced, newly invented tipples, or expensive wines, or designer beers, but will fail to spot the attractions of a modest goldie with a dash of good old Scottish tap, or even – with a nod to these transatlantic times – swirled gently round the rocks?

It can't surely be because, as we know, women have, on account of their build and chemical make-up, a lower tolerance for alcohol. For while women are assuredly less able to take too much of the hard stuff, a night on the readymix cocktail circuit is certainly not about to do their livers any better favours. Neither would most women confess to a secret desire to grow their own beer belly.

That women are no strangers to bottled Scottish pleasures is quite evident from any cursory examination of the whisky industry's history. From the weaver to the Highland landlady, from the country-house hostess to several generations of the British royal family there is considerable evidence to suggest that whilst the men were out doing whatever it is men do, the women rarely felt obliged to find solace in a glass of warm milk.

(Though it has to be conceded at this juncture that Queen Victoria never quite got the hang of the stuff. Despite guided tours of several distilleries, despite being credited with introducing the whisky habit to Balmoral-bound southern gentry steeped in claret, her own preferences proved just a wee thing idiosyncratic. Rumour has it that she not only felt able to pour some famous labels into her afternoon tea, but also into her dinner wine – a variation on the gastronomic theme which could have done little for either brew. She was also, it appears, more than tolerant of the fact that some of the men in her life, notably John Brown, were capable of trying some of the local vintages, so assiduously, that they could not always be counted upon to pledge fresh allegiance to the throne much before lunchtime on the morning after the tasting before. Her Majesty, it seems, was constructed of sterner stuff: your national monarch, made from girders.)

Yet regardless of the sturdiness of their constitution, or their admitted fondness for a glass that cheers, there are many arenas where whisky figures largely in the proceedings, which are, quite simply, off limits to women. Prominent among those is the stag Burns supper where even the chieftain of the pudden race is well doused in the stuff, although at many of these occasions, as wives of returning revellers have witnessed, the food would appear to have been an entirely optional extra. There is a significant difference between all-male and mixed tributes to the bard. At the male supper Mr Burns is used as an appropriate occasion for compulsory over-indulgence with occasional forays into poetry, philosophy and polemic. At those gatherings where all sections of the human race rate admission, poetry, song and literature are used as the basis for intermittent over-indulgence.

Whisky and freedom may gang thegither, but the freedom of women to drink whisky is sometimes dependent on the distance mine host has contrived to travel from neanderthal times.

Still, those women excluded from the proceedings on or around 25 January may console themselves with the thought that many of the gallants who have spent the last half dozen hours in ringing declarations of international brotherhood and the rights of man will almost certainly metamorphose into wee sleekit cowrin' timorous beasties should they be ill-advised enough to turn up on their own doorsteps at 3 a.m. without their house keys. In such a familiar domestic scenario women do, of course, feel free to give their own speechmaking prowess a pretty free rein. But you may assume whatever they choose to say, it will not be *Slainte*.

We'll wrap it in tartan,' said the marketing man, 'that's a powerful puller in this price range.' He was talking about shortbread but it could equally well have been Dundee cake, whisky-flavoured marmalade, Edinburgh rock, haggis, smoked salmon or a can of cock-a-leekie soup.

I was eavesdropping in the offices of a Scottish food company as the executives talked through their projections for the coming year. Did packaging food in a nostalgic manner really work? And what did images of heather, foaming burns and clan warriors add to the taste and flavour of the contents of the packets and tins?

I came away a bit bemused. Where had this strange notion come from that a kilted Highlander waving a sword could sell toffees? An ad agency in London? Or was it some misconception in the Scottish subconscious that there had once been a Golden Age when everyone from the laird down to the humblest peasant lived the good life taking food for free from rivers and lochs and woods and forests?

In reality there was a clearly defined pecking order; being a member of a clan didn't entitle you to live high on the hog. At Lord Lovat's seat at Dounie Castle, the neighbouring chiefs and distinguished guests were offered French cuisine and good claret; lower down the table humbler folk were given beef and mutton with a jug of lesser wine while the commoners of the clan at the foot of the table picked at a sheep's head and drank whisky.

Memoirs and recollections of the pre-industrial age, being largely written by the well-heeled, reinforce the myth of universal largesse. 'Game was plentiful,' recalled Elizabeth Grant of Rothiemurchus, 'red-deer, roe, hares, grouse, ptarmigan and partridge; the rivers provided trout and salmon, the different lochs pike and char; the garden abounded in common fruit and common vegetables; cranberries and raspberries ran over the country and the poultry yard was ever well furnished.'

The joys of the big house where the butler announced dinner in Gaelic – *'Tha am biadh airleadh le bhur cead a bhaintighearna'* (the food is on the table, by your leave, my lady) – is richly documented by Osgood Mackenzie of Inverewe drawing on his own memoirs and those of his uncle, Dr John Mackenzie. His ancestral home at Conon was like a Highland branch of Fortnum & Mason's: 'There were jam-pots by the hundreds of every sort, shelves of preserved candied apricots and Magnum Bonum plums. Smoked sheep and deer tongues were also there and from the roof hung strings of threaded artichoke bottoms dried for putting into soups.'

Every year his grandmother and her servants made

gooseberry and currant wines, raspberry vinegar, spruce and ginger beer. The gardens grew peaches, cherries, nectarines, grapes and filberts. And in June 'we never failed to have a big china bowl after dinner with a pail of cream to wash down the first strawberries of the season'. On the table were Madeira, sherry, port and sundry wines of the best vintages that could be procured.

This arcadian picture of the Scottish larder is perpetuated in the journal of Faujus de Saint Fond, the French naturalist who made a jaunt to Scotland in 1784. Even in the wildest islands of the west, elegance, gentility and gastronomic delight abounded. On Mull, at the house of Maclean of Torloisk, he sat down to a dinner so lavish that he recorded it in great detail. There was broth, black pudding made with bullock's blood and barley flour seasoned with pepper and ginger, broiled beef, roast mutton and potatoes steeped in the juice, pickled cucumbers and ginger, milk prepared in a variety of ways, puddings made of barley-cream and raisins and two different kinds of cheese. On other days there would have been heath-cocks and woodcocks or waterfowl, depending on the luck of the chase.

And oh, the breakfasts! John Knox, a London bookseller on safari at about the same time, when staying with the Highland gentry would come down in the morning to French rolls, oat and barley bread, honey in the comb, red and blackcurrant jellies, marmalade, butter fresh and salted, fresh eggs, fresh and salted herring, haddocks and whiting, cold rounds of venison, beef and mutton hams and a choice of tea or coffee.

And when the traveller finally made his way back to Edinburgh in the Age of Enlightenment he found dinners and suppers unrivalled in Britain. Epicureans like David Hume, Adam Smith, Lord Monboddo, Henry Cockburn, Francis Jeffrey, the Ballantyne brothers and Walter Scott himself drew their gastronomic inspiration from fine local ingredients, imported delicacies and the European culinary heritage.

Hume had first discovered the joy of food when he was despatched for reasons of health to France at the age of 23. Later in life he held an unofficial position in the embassy in Paris and became a noted amateur cook and *bon viveur*. The civilising influence of food and conversation reached its Scottish peak in those heady days when the Athens of the North was also its Burgundy and its Bordeaux.

If one listed only half of the dishes Meg Dods proposed for a festivity like St Andrew's Day you'd see the richness and the variety of Scottish upper-crust cuisine: potted game, minced collops, salt cod with egg sauce, crimped skate, smoked tongue, salt Caithness goose, sheep's head broth, haunch of venison with wine sauce, posset, blancmange and apple puddings. At its best the diet of upper- and middle-class Scots in the 19th century was substantial and by today's standards highly enviable. But there was a downside. While the local gourmets were dining at the fictional Cleikum Inn on hare soup, stewed red trout, pullet braised and served with rice and mushroom sauce, cranberry tart and cream, others did less well.

In his *Walks in Edinburgh*, published in 1825, Robert Chambers describes how he was conducted into a smoky den 'where about 20 Scotch Drovers were regaling themselves with whisky and potatoes'. This was frugal fare, unlikely to raise the spirits or promote the therapy of enjoyment. It was all too common, particularly in those parts of the country where subsistence farming produced subsistence fare. Some lived well, most endured a diet distinguished mainly by its monotony. 'Oatmeal with milk, which they cook in different ways, is their constant food, three times a day, throughout the year, Sundays and holidays included,' wrote J. Donaldson of the peasants who lived in the Carse of Gowrie.

Travellers like Dorothy Wordsworth observed this culinary poverty much as they might have observed the cooking in African kraals, but it wasn't until the members of the Napier Commission embarked in 1883 on their investigation of the complaints of the crofters in the Highlands and Islands that the rest of Britain became aware how poorly fed thousands of native Scots were. Their diet, particularly in times of famine and crop failure, was bleak.

'Our staple food is meal, potatoes, fish when it's got, our only drink being tea,' attested John Macpherson of Milovaig in Skye. In Lewis, milk and butter were scarce. In Shetland some families without a cow turned to buying syrup for their children. Duncan Macrae, an old man of 87 living north of Dornie on Loch Long, remembered as a child that people had milk and 'the produce of sheep, goats, cows, cattle and fish. Now they are fed on potatoes and herring, bread and tea, but they have no butter and no cheese.' There were similar complaints on Foula, where in winter in place of milk the children were given sugar and water. For dinner they might have fish and potatoes 'but they are not potatoes: you could wring the water out of them'.

Most of the energy of these people was directed towards survival – no time for the indulgence of culinary creativity. Near Durness, Alexander Morrison told the Commissioners that there was not a single horse in the township to lighten the burden of agriculture: 'A man must go first to the seaware and then to the spade; he must sow the seed and then harrow the ground after that and go three-quarters of a mile up the hill for a creel of peat to make a fire that will make ready his breakfast.'

The destitution of the crofters and cottars was rendered more poignant by the incomparably beautiful landscape in which they tried to eke out a living. The sunsets, the heathered glens, the romantic lochs look good on chocolate boxes, but these devastated acres failed to produce a heritage of fine cooking.

Those who emigrated to the slums of Glasgow from the Hebrides took no indigenous culinary heritage with them; malnutrition and rickets became endemic. No happy memories of abundance there. It is a legacy which is reflected in the widespread availability of factory food in Scotland. Where there was no native skill in food preparation the packets and tins took over.

The English and the Scots have been great borrowers. The pre-eminence of French and, to a lesser extent, Italian chefs in our hotels and restaurants reflects less our indifference to food than the astonishingly rich culinary culture of France and Italy.

Four-fifths of the Scottish population live in towns; even to this day the French remain solidly attached to a countryside brimming with good food and wine. The move to convenience food may be well under way but it was still possible in 1991 for the food writer Anne Willan to explore ten different regions of France and find a wealth of fine ingredients and traditional dishes. 'Little more than an hour from Notre Dame,' she writes in *La France Gastronomique*, 'you'll still find peasants living off the land, growing their own fruit and vegetables, raising rabbits, poultry and eggs, brewing wine or cider and "eau-de-vie", the water of life.' She writes lyrically of lavender honey, truffles and foie gras, walnut oil, *champignons* and *charcuterie*, fine cheeses and a profusion of garlic, wild herbs and bread made by bakers who rise happily at 4 a.m. to give their dough the long, slow rising essential for flavour.

Visitors to Alsace, the Loire, Provence, Périgord, Gascony and Languedoc will still find the distinctive dishes of those areas. Tourists searching for similar evidence of regional cuisine in the Scottish countryside are likely to be disappointed. Although there has been a spirited renascence of cheese-making on a few small farms, a welcome outbreak of home baking in village halls and a great building of smokehouses to add value to the glut of farmed salmon, the solid roots of Scottish cooking are not always easy to find.

Cafés and restaurants which rely on frozen food from the large catering companies quite often end up reheating inferior imitations of foreign dishes for bewildered foreign visitors. Italians are presented with menus offering *pizza* and *lasagne*, Spaniards are plied with boil-in-the-bag *paella* and the French pick curiously at miserable versions of *coq au vin* and *boeuf bourguignon*. The nearest they might get to something indisputably Scottish is haggis and chips or a reconstituted soup mix labelled Scotch broth.

The Scottish Tourist Board has for years conducted a valiant campaign to give hotel and restaurant menus a more conspicuously 'local' flavour. Guesthouse proprietors and bed and breakfast ladies have been provided with a manual which enables them to present dishes which, from the title at least, can lay a claim, however spurious, to being regional. Semiotic rather than authentic, the recipes attach topographical markers where they don't legitimately belong. In the manual you'll find Aboyne Fruit Tart, Angus Fish Soup, Auld Reekie Pheasant Casserole, Baked Trout Kinross and Carse of Gowrie fruit salad, as if such things had been a part of the gastronomy in those parts from olden times. Other dishes devised by the STB to impart echoes of a bogus culinary culture lean heavily on the heather-and-tartan sales promotion kit.

My favourites in this department are Balmoral Tripe (a favourite of Landseer?), Steak Bonnie Prince Charlie, Dream of Rob Roy, Heilan' Steaks and Rannoch Venison Steak as in

> Sure, by Tummel an' Loch Rannoch an' Lochaber
>   I will go,
> By heather tracks wi' heaven in their wiles,
> It's the far Coolins that are puttin' love on me,
> As step I wi' my cromak to the Isles.

Come to think of it, if you can foist Rannoch Venison Steaks on unsuspecting tourists, why not Tummel Tattie Pot wi' wee chappit chippies, Lochaber Crofter's Omelette and Coolin salad or Cromak Cranachan wi' a gey drap o' Tartan Mist?

When you arrive at the stage of having to invent a gastronomy you might well believe that all is lost. Certainly an enormous number of recipes documented by writers like F. Marian McNeill and Elizabeth Craig have failed to survive in contemporary kitchens and restaurants.

Go to Lewis, Barra, or anywhere in the Northern Isles and you'll find the same convenience foods in the local shops as you do on the mainland. Nowhere in Europe has convenience food been assimilated more enthusiastically than in Scotland. It's sad to go to Shetland and see in the supermarkets all those imported processed foods on an island which a hundred years ago had its own highly individual ways of preparing meat and fish. There was, for instance, a repertoire of dishes based on fish livers – muggies, stap, slot, burstin, krappin, krus and sangster.

On my first visit to Shetland I looked for any evidence of a native cuisine and predictably found nothing in the shops but Kellogg's cornflakes, Heinz tinned soups and

Birdseye fishfingers. In the tourist office I was directed to the council house where lived Rhoda Bulter, poet and keeper of memories. New fishing technology, she told me, had destroyed the old fish recipes. 'Except a privately owned boat goes to the fishing we don't get the livers now because the fish are all gutted at sea and the innards are dumped.' Rhoda reckoned the oil boom hadn't done a great deal for Shetland 'other than to make people realise just what was slipping through their fingers – like their dialect and their diet'.

Many of Rhoda's poems celebrate foods that are now no more than a memory – the reestit mutton, which was pickled and hung in the chimney beside the peat fire, and bland, the fermented whey which sparkled in your glass like champagne. In her poem 'Maet Noo an Dan' she rages gently against the factory rubbish that has invaded Shetland and recalls the lost delights of her childhood:

> An can you mind da brose and bursteen, rossen
>   sparrels and heads taw swee,
> Da liver heads an oily muggies, stap and crappin,
>   fish and gree;
> Sookit pilticks, purled tatties, an treckle dumplins
>   in a cloot;
> A piece a hirkie wi a bannock, muckles hufsies
>   tick wi fruit
> An ta slake your trist whin casting paets or
>   harrowin rigs or siftin anns
> You hed nae fizz lemonade or pepsi cola oota cans
>   . . .
> . . . O my! Whaat wid I gie eenoo for tattie soup
>   wi reestit mutton.

What has been lost over the years in rural places is the ability to produce simple foods which were years ago a commonplace. I'm thinking of nothing more complicated than crowdie. In the days when every croft or farm kept at least one cow, a bowl of it was always on the table. Homemade crowdie is now as rare as home-churned butter, farmyard eggs and the vegetable patch. The herring fishery has been almost destroyed and the last fish have been scoured up from every loch and voe. Conservationists are predicting that unless stringent regulations are adopted we shall destroy our shellfish resources too.

We can still talk of Scotland's larder – the grouse, salmon and the venison – but for how long? In the eyes of the public relations man there is no difference between the free-ranging wild salmon and the artificially fed caged variety; nor for that matter do supermarkets distinguish between deer shot in the wilderness and those reared domestically.

The more artificial food becomes the more anxious manufacturers are to distance themselves from the mass-produced, factory image of modern technology. Although the shortbread or the pies may come from a hygienic, automated complex on some industrial estate, the advertising and the packaging make coy references to a simple and more innocent age. Evocative references to farmhouses and dairies position ice-cream in the countryside not in the town. Honey must come from bees that hovered over the heather moors; pies are made a 'traditional' receipt. Only the list of additives gives the game away.

To cater for discriminating and affluent consumers suspicious of junk food, restaurants and country hotels have sprung up in the last two decades specialising in fruit, vegetables, fish and meat which is above average in quality. The move to more wholesome food, to tomatoes with some flavour and poultry which has not been intensively farmed, is paralleled by the growing interest in malt whisky. Whisky is the textbook example of a product which has been upholstered with so many myths that most people assume it has always played a basic role in Scottish life.

But as Billy Kay and Cailean Maclean prove in their book about the Scottish love affair with wine, *Knee Deep in Claret* (Mainstream, 1983), the popular notion of whisky as the drink of Celtic civilisation, although carefully fostered by the industry, lacks historical substance. 'Gaelic songs, poetry and oral tradition,' they write, 'make mention of wine literally centuries before whisky makes a similar appearance.' Wine and brandy were the tipples of the clan chiefs in the 16th and 17th centuries, not whisky. So ruinous was the consumption of wine in the islands that in 1616 the Scottish Privy Council was moved to severely restrict its sale and consumption.

The fireside stories of marathon drinking sessions centre on claret, not *uisge beatha*. To prove their manhood on coming of age it was claret that future Macleod chiefs were required to drink from the historic Dunvegan ox horn – one and a half pints of it in a single draught.

Supermarket sales suggest that the favourite spirit of the Scots isn't whisky at all but vodka. Export statistics confirm that more of The Glenlivet is drunk in Italy than on its native heath and that fine malt whisky is more enthusiastically appreciated in New York than in New Lanark. It's all very confusing.

Romantic writers like Neil Gunn and Maurice Walsh fostered the erroneous idea that whisky had been part of the fabric of society from post-Viking days. Another tireless advocate of the pre-eminence of whisky in Scottish culture was Aeneas Macdonald, who wrote of 'the vanished age of gold when the vintages of the north had their students and lovers'. In those halcyon days 'whisky still held its place in the cellars of the gentry and of men of letters who selected it with as much care and knowledge as they gave to the stocking of their cellars with claret'.

I wonder. Whisky certainly never penetrated into the kitchen except possibly as a pick-me-up for the cook. I can find no traditional recipes which call for infusions of whisky. To remedy this lacuna, cookery writer Rosalie Gow compiled in 1990 a book of what she called '100 Luxury Recipes' involving various amounts of whisky. There was little, she found, that could not be given a whisky fix from Camembert croquettes to glazed *poussins* and bread and butter pudding. Amounts recommended varied from a quarter of a pint in a casserole of beef to just a wee sensation in a banana brûlée.

There is a more enduring future for Scottish gastronomy than whipping the odd spoonful of whisky into a cranachan. What has been emerging in the last few years is a new style of cooking in which good ingredients, often from local waters or farms, are allowed to speak for themselves. The new breed of cooks is uninhibited: they borrow from Asia, from Europe and from the Americas. Their food is likely to use both oatmeal and olive oil, wrap salmon in seaweed, marry chanterelles with lamb and nettles with Brie, put pickled ginger in a watercress sauce, bake oysters with red peppers.

On Shetland you'll find homemade nut and herb bread accompanying a classic Scandinavian egg and anchovy dish; on the west coast Mallaig scallops with a Barsac sauce; bouillabaisse in Fort William; crab with tomato and garlic mayonnaise on Skye; in Kingussie mousseline of local pike; near Aberfeldy charlotte of grouse with blueberry sauce.

Nothing to do with Bonnie Prince Charlie or your Heilan' granny there. No need to put a tartan border round the menu. This is a cuisine that puts the emphasis on fresh and seasonal ingredients, a welcome backlash to the old style cooking which relied far too much on tired dishes from catering colleges.

This is food you have to seek out; it's still swamped by the smell of heavy-duty frying oil and the chip pan, the culinary equivalent of whisky-and-lemonade, but its emergence parallels the growing interest in fine malts. Quality outperforms quantity every time – food may well be fuel but it should also be fun and as much an occasion for joy as piping, dancing, poetry or any other expression of a country's cultural strength and exuberance.

Of all the processes involved in the production of whisky, the one most shrouded in mystery is that of maturation. The clear, harsh and pungent new spirit is placed in a wooden container which is locked away in the dark in a cold damp warehouse. By some strange alchemy, a transformation takes place and the spirit emerges some years later, golden coloured, mellow and flavoursome, as if by magic, or so the advertising people would have us believe.

There is another view of the maturation process: that it is merely a series of complex chemical reactions, aided by oxidation, evaporation and extraction mechanisms. The lengthy period required for these reactions to come to fruition is due to the low temperature and to the very wide physical dispersion of the relevant molecules within the cask. This is the scientific viewpoint. Naturally a purely scientific description would not read so well as 'aged in oaken wood' (note the antiquarian terminology), or 'caressed by the seaweed-scented breezes' or 'wafted by the pine-laden air of the Cairngorms for its lengthy slumber in sherrywood'.

Although there is no harm in the advertisers' language, the attribution of mystical properties does not help understanding. It is a pity that for a very long time, the drinking public has known little of the cask's critical role in the transformation of distillate to whisky and discussion has been on a very slender knowledge of the facts. Much is made of the influence of water, barley malt, peat and pot-stills in articles, books and advertising, yet little has been said about the function of the cask. Recently, however, there have been signs that the importance of the type of wood used with a particular whisky has been given greater recognition – witness Macallan, which has advertised its adherence to sherry casks, and Glenmorangie their use of ex-bourbon casks.

In 1984, the Scotch Malt Whisky Society pioneered the bottling of single casks, and its bottlings have shown the variety and individuality which are to be found among malt whiskies taken from individual carefully chosen casks. The taste of any given whisky varies greatly, according to whether it is bottled in plain oak, sherry or bourbon cask, and different sherries as well as different bourbons will impart a variety of flavours to the whiskies which are matured in their erstwhile containers. Whiskies mature more or less rapidly, depending on the type of cask used and the warehouse conditions of maturation. Beyond a certain point, however, there is no necessary connection between age and quality.

In their knowledge of how their tipple is made, whisky drinkers compare poorly with wine drinkers. The wine industry, unlike the whisky distillers, had made great use in its advertising of the importance of grape varieties, soil type, vintages, casks, maturation and how these affect product character. Wine drinkers clearly have almost as great a thirst for knowledge as they do for wine.

In the last decade, beer drinkers have become dissatisfied with the limited variety of beers on offer, and have sought out different styles of beer, of which there are great numbers. Thus regional cask ales, Gueze and Lambic beers, wheat beers, fruit beers and genuine Pilsner beers from Czechoslovakia are all coming to be more widely known and consumed. One need only recall the ubiquitous Nicolas or the Watney Red Barrel which used to dominate the market for wine and beers respectively in the UK, to notice the changes which have taken place. There is a growing consumer awareness of original and unique products, and their characteristic flavours. The growth of demand for malt whisky mirrors this.

In Scotch whisky, the regional influence on flavour has often been described – Islay, Speyside, Northern and Lowland whiskies have typical characteristics which are sought by blenders and consumers. By contrast, the part played by the cask in determining individuality of flavour has been little discussed. In this chapter we will consider the use of the cask and its influence on flavour.

The use of wooden casks as containers can be traced back some 5,000 years. In the Book of Kings, 17 and 18, reference is made to a barrel of meal and four barrels of water, thus the use of wooden casks for storage of dry and wet goods. Previous to this, hollowed-out logs with animal hide ends were used. The reasons for the development of wooden casks as containers are not hard to find. Casks are extremely strong and they last for a number of trips; they are easily handled, one man being able to move a cask even when loaded with several hundred pounds' weight. (A full cask can be turned and guided in any direction because it can be pivoted on a small contact point.) The use of casks in the transportation of Scotch whisky was therefore a natural development.

The value of the cask in modifying the flavour of newly distilled spirit was probably first noted in the 17th century. In such times the newly distilled spirit would have been a harsh, poorly flavoured product, whose worst characteristics were disguised by using flavourings such as blackberry, raspberry and juniper during the distillation. The discovery of the flavour-enhancing properties of oak containers was probably accidental. The origins of whisky and gin products which we know today can be traced back to early attempts to alter and improve the flavour of the distilled spirit. A spirit still exists in Holland, known as Oude Genevre, which has many similarities to some of the early products. It is produced using a spirit made from a cereal mash which includes malted barley. The spirit has characteristics not unlike those of a lightly flavoured new malt whisky. During distillation, juniper, coriander and various other botanicals are added to give the characteristic gin flavour. In contrast, modern gins use completely neutral, flavourless alcohol as the base. This was a late 19th-century development. (Both turpentine and sulphuric acid were at one time added to give flavour. The consequences of this can be seen in Hogarth prints of Gin Lane.)

Scientific investigations into maturation started in the late 19th century. Despite the very limited resources and techniques then available, findings were made which are still fundamental to the understanding of the process of maturation. It was shown that a selective absorption of whisky components took place within the wood, and the action of the wood was not merely physical; some chemical changes also took place. Aldehydes other than acetaldehyde, as well as compounds derived solely from the wood, contributed to the maturation process, and the type of cask and the condition of warehousing considerably influenced the course of maturation. Analytical details of grain, Speyside, Islay and Lowland whiskies supported many of these observations and tests were carried out for extract, ash, total volatile and non-volatile acids, ethers, higher alcohol aldehydes and pure furfural. These basic tests supported observations which are now being confirmed by the more sophisticated analytical techniques available to today's scientists.

In an excellent practical paper to the Scottish section of the Institute of Brewing in 1906, on 'Casks, their manufacture & treatment', Haldane discussed the need for control of cask quality and showed how this could be achieved through standardisation. Some interesting comments were made on sherry casks and how these could be fraudulently manufactured by unscrupulous traders who shipped worn-out casks from Leith to Spain, rinsed them with sherry, covered them with cobwebs and allowed them to lie around in the bodega to acquire a patina of age. The casks were sold back to the Scotch whisky industry at an inflated price.

Oak wood is used in cooperage for its hardness, its flexibility, its impermeability and its extractable compounds. There are many varieties of oak, but only a few such as the pendunculate oak, the sessile oak in Europe and the white oak in America are used in the manufacture of casks for mellowing spirit. Oaks belong to the genus *Quercus* and those used in cooperage wood are *Quercus Robur* or common English oak, *Quercus Petraea* – a sessile oak found in France and northern Spain – and *Quercus Alba*, a white oak from North America. In France the *Quercus Robur* used for spirit originates mainly from the Limousin forest, with lesser amounts of *Quercus Petraea* from Troncais and Gascony. Wood for casks for Scotch whisky is imported from France, Spain or the United States of America. The American white oak is grown mainly in Missouri, Kentucky and Arkansas. The heartwood is the most valuable part of white oak timber because it is compressed by growth and the cell walls are thick and hard. The heartwood is surrounded by sapwood, which during the tree's growth changes into hardwood. After it is cut, sapwood can be made usable by careful seasoning. The heartwood of American oak is made up of the following:

Cellulose	49–52%
Lignin	31–33%
Hemicellulose	22%
Other extractables	7–11%

European oaks are similar in composition.

One of the most important features of the conversion of sapwood into heartwood is the formation of tyloses. This involves a swelling of the cell walls during spring growth, which renders the timber impermeable to liquids. Not all species of oak exhibit this phenomenon and where they do not, the timber will be porous and therefore unsuitable for maturation. Tylose formation varies from season to season. American oak generally possesses a higher proportion of tylose than do European oaks.

In France, Armagnac is matured in Gascony oak casks and Cognac in Limousin oak. The French practice is to mature both spirits and wines in new oak casks for a few months prior to longer maturation in used wood. In Spain, American oak is customarily used for fine and amontillado sherries, and Spanish oak for olosoro. In the maturation of Scotch whisky, a variety of different types and sizes of casks is used. Since all of these impart their own characteristic maturation patterns to the spirit, it is desirable that the differences are understood.

Harsh, pungent, new spirit undergoes a metamorphosis and becomes mellow and drinkable. Several factors are at work to produce this, including the production of the distillate, the type of cask used and the conditions in which the casks are warehoused. The distillate varies from bland grain spirit to full-bodied malt, which is dependent on the type of malted barley used, the degree of peating and the conditions of fermentation and distillation.

The nature of the wood surface in contact with the spirit is variable. At one extreme is the exhausted, non-active, low-extract surface of a much-filled cask and, at the other, that of a highly active, first-fill cask which has a high extract reservoir. The nature of the surface depends on the *Quercus* species used, how the wood has been treated (charred, sherry, etc.), and the number of times the cask has been used. It is possible to combine selected distillate types with particular cask characteristics to yield a unique flavour profile.

The main types of cask used in Scotland can be summarised as follows:

	Contents in litres	*Surface: Volume ratio*
American standard barrel	191	100
Dump hogshead	254	89
Dump puncheon	463	72
Butt	500	71
Puncheon	558	68

The principal fermentation of flavour is the surface-to-volume ratio. In ideal conditions, using casks of the same wood type and history, a smaller cask with a higher surface-to-volume ratio will mature the whisky in a shorter period of time.

Various treatment techniques are used by the distiller to determine the character of the mature whisky. The main techniques are thermal degradation, sherry treatment and wine seasoning.

In the United States, Spain and Scotland, the internal surface of the cask is charred. The degree of charring varies, depending on the use to which the cask is to be put. Casks used for the maturation of bourbon whisky are heavily charred. It is a legal requirement in the USA that the casks be used only once. After being used once, the casks are broken down and transported to Scotland where they are reassembled, to be used for malt spirit. The first fill with bourbon removes the heavy, woody, vanilla characteristics from the charred surface. In subsequent fillings, the more delicate malt whiskies acquire a subtler concentration of these flavours.

The reactions which take place during charring are extremely complex and not yet fully understood. It is likely that the layer of active carbon in the charred wood assists in removing some unwanted compounds from the whisky. Charring also begins the process of lignin decomposition which leads to the more rapid release of compounds such as aromatic aldehydes into the whisky.

In sherry treatment, casks are usually 500-litre butts manufactured in Spain from Spanish oak. Initially, the cask is seasoned by the grape fermentation process and it is then used as a container to ship matured sherries to the UK. It is likely that during its use as a fermentation vessel, some degradation of the inner wood surface will take place. This allows the mature sherry more fully to permeate the inner surface of the cask. Once the cask is emptied of sherry, and refilled with spirit, the sherry absorbed in the wood migrates slowly into the maturing spirit. Some decomposition of the lignin, similar to the effect of charring, may also result from this treatment.

Sherry is now more commonly shipped in stainless steel tanks than in oak casks, with the result that there are fewer casks available for whisky maturation. In both Spain and the UK, methods have been devised to simulate the sherry-cask seasoning process, with varying degrees of success. Remarkably, one of these was a steam and ammonia treatment, developed by Señor Gomez of M.M. Gomez in Spain. American oak casks were treated with steam and ammonia under high pressure. This did little but strip the tannins from the inside of the cask. Whiskies kept in such casks derived virtually no benefit and showed very few of the maturation characteristics which were expected.

In wine seasoning, casks are used for grape fermentation and then filled with maturing sherry, which is left in the cask for varying periods. The sherry is poured out and the casks shipped empty to Scotland. This treatment has proved to be fairly effective.

In 1888, a patented apparatus was introduced by W.P. Lowrie. This device used pressurised steam to test and season casks. The procedure has developed into the present wine treatment process, in which a very dark, sweet sherry known as Paxarette is introduced into the cask, which is then pressurised for about ten minutes. Following this the excess sherry is discharged. The process has the effect of forcing the sherry into the pores of the oak. It gives a flavour of sherry, thought it must be admitted that the flavour is not of the order of a newly filled sherry cask.

The number of times the cask has been filled greatly influences the result of maturation. Since only a finite quantity of extractives is present in the cask, and these are removed over several fillings, there is a gradual decline in their influence on the spirit. After having been used several times to mature spirit, a cask may still be a sound container, but have a negligible ability to mature whisky.

This can be measured. The following table shows the result of a comparison of six standard hogsheads, all ten years old, filled with the same distillate. It can be seen from the chemical analysis and the sensory reports that there is a correlation between increasing levels of component concentration and the whisky's appeal to the senses.

Effect of casks on the maturation of Scotch Whisky

Cask sample	*Colour (A 490 run)*	*Acids*	*Tannins*	*Galloyl esters*	*Hexoros*	*Sensory analysis*
1	3.1	31.3	12.8	1.0	19.2	Immature/ greasy
2	7.8	43.5	20.9	5.6	17.4	Immature/ greasy
3	10.9	48.1	27.7	11.6	19.2	Slightly mature and woody
4	14.1	51.8	35.1	25.2	22.7	Slightly mature and woody
5	15.6	55.6	38.8	37.2	26.7	Fully mature
6	17.2	56.0	38.8	37.0	35.4	Fully mature/ rich

There is a process used to rejuvenate casks which has been found to be successful. The ends of sound but worn-out casks are removed. The interior of the cask is steamed and scraped and the cask is then put over a gas burner which ignites any spirit evaporating from the wood. Once the spirit is burnt off and the wood dry, the wood itself ignites. The blue flame of the burning alcohol turns yellow as the wood burns. After a time, the gas flame is turned off and the wood allowed to burn on its own. The time of this burning is controlled with a view to maximising the formation of aromatic aldehydes. This process, if combined with wine treatment, gives maturation characteristics which are very close to those of a cask fresh from sherry use.

In times past, casks were often damaged in handling. They had to be repaired and the new wood thus introduced prolonged the cask's useful life as a vehicle for maturation. Because such repairs are now rare, thanks to mechanical handling, it has become necessary for a system of cask classification to be developed, which enables the cask's ability to mature spirit to be ascertained. Records are kept throughout the cask's life which detail the number and length of fillings, the types of whisky matured, the location of the maturations and any repairs carried out.

It will be obvious from the foregoing that mere length of time in cask is no indicator of the degree of maturity of a whisky. When malt whiskies are bottled, the blender must mix together whiskies from many different casks in order to achieve a product which is consistent in the qualities it displays to the palate of the discerning drinker.

Over the years, the principal mechanisms of maturation in oak casks have become well known. These mechanisms are common to all distilled spirits which are matured in oak casks. The mechanisms are the breakdown of the various polymers of wood and their subsequent transition into the ageing whisky; reactions between the extracted wood components and distillate congeners; and reactions among distillate congeners.

Wood components are extracted directly by the alcohol. These wood components, from the heartwood, contain cellulose, lignin, hemicellulose and an extractable fraction consisting of volatile oils, volatile and non-volatile acids, sugars, steroids, tannic substances, pigments and inorganic compounds. Over 100 volatile components have been identified in oak-wood shavings, among the most important of which are the isomeric 3-methyl-4-octanolides which are named Quercus Lactone – A and B, or oak lactones, as they are commonly known. These compounds are to be found in different proportions in different oak species, and tend to be highest in *Quercus Alba*.

A process of decomposition takes place during charring and to some extent with the sherry treatment, involving the macro molecules which form the framework of wood, such as lignin, cellulose and hemicellulose. This process is followed by elution into the spirit. Lignin-related compounds are among the most significant groups and they are closely associated with the development of mature whisky flavour. They include vanillin, syringaldehyde, coniferaldeyhyde and p-hydroxybenzaldehyde. They are to be found in differing proportions in all distilled spirits matured in casks. Lignin products are to be found in much higher concentrations in charred casks than in uncharred casks. Many of the aromatic aldehydes are important flavour characteristics and they make up some of the flavour characteristics of the mature spirit. Some of the wood components react with components of the unaged distillates, modifying some of the more unpleasant characteristics of the new spirit.

Various hexose sugars as well as glycerol originate in the oak wood. Over the period of maturation, sugars such as arabinose, glucose, xylose and galactose are produced, most rapidly in the first year. The rate of formation of fructose and glycerol on the other hand increases with age, as the hemicellulose breaks down. These compounds are likely to contribute sweet flavours to the whisky. By no means are all of the oak wood reactions beneficial; some can cause instability and others lead to a cloudiness in the whisky once bottled.

Reactions involving only the distillate components also take place. These are the reactions which increase the prevalence of aldehydes and esters, which produce more pronounced floral, fruity, leafy and spicy characteristics in the mature spirit.

The distiller can influence the rate of maturation by varying the strength of the alcohol filled into the cask. Since the 19th century it has been known that maturation proceeds more slowly at higher strengths. The most commonly used strength today is 63.4 per cent alcohol by volume.

It has been found that warehouse temperature and, to a lesser extent, humidity can affect the extraction of non-volatile components derived from the wood, so some control over flavour characteristics can be exercised in the warehouse. Though these effects are not large, they can be significant. Until 25 years ago, almost all whisky was matured in stone-built, single- or multi-storey warehouses located beside the distillery. The single-storey warehouses had cinder floors and in the multi-storey warehouses the floors were of wood. Casks were stored in stows, usually two or three high, sitting on wooden runners placed on the casks beneath. The warehouses were often very damp and such conditions were reputed to produce the best whiskies. This was thought to be especially appropriate to sherry butts. Warehouses today tend to be larger than before and have brick or metal walls and alloy roofs. Steel racking allows casks to be stored up to ten high.

Evaporation of the low-boiling compounds through the wood of the cask is one of the better-recognised phenomena. This is when the angels get their share. Ethanol and water are lost due to diffusion through the cask staves and the cask head, and by subsequent evaporation into the atmosphere. The alcohol content of spirits in a cask increases during ageing under conditions of low-to-moderate relative humidity, but decreases under conditions of high humidity. During ageing in the unheated, humid warehouses of Scotland, the proof strength goes down; in the warmer, drier conditions prevailing in a warehouse in the United States, proof strength goes up during storage. There is widespread belief that Scotch malt whiskies mature best in cold, damp warehouses, though research has not entirely supported this view.

In the whisky industry, systems for describing the taste and smell of whisky have been developed, which use terms standardised against particular chemical compounds. Staff are trained to use these terms together with scales of intensity to describe whiskies. By using statistical methods, principal components of whiskies can be analysed and two- and three-dimensional models produced which show precisely the relationships among the constituents of the whisky. Such modelling has proved useful in assessing the results of maturation.

Obviously, research in the industry has concentrated on the more commonly available types of cask. However, one does from time to time come across whisky matured in casks which have been used for other things. Port, Madeira, rum and brandy all impart characteristics of their own, not all by any means desirable. Casks which have previously held jam and fruit have reportedly been used, though the results of this are not known to the writer.

With second-fill casks and those used more often, the type of whisky which occupied the cask for the preceding period of maturation will exert an influence on the maturing whisky. Thus a cask which has held a peaty Islay whisky will not in general be used in its next filling to mature a delicate Speyside.

That the single most important determinant of

flavour in a malt whisky is the cask, has been shown by both sensory and scientific investigation. Such investigations have sought to attribute sensory descriptions to as many as possible of the 800 compounds so far identified in malt whisky. It must be admitted that at the time of writing, this enterprise has met with relatively little success. Scotch whisky is extremely complex and its analysis in the terms described has a long way to go.

Flavour results not only from individual compounds but from conjunctions of compounds and of groups of compounds, and different ratios of those conjunctions produce different effects. Some compounds are present in too small concentrations to be detected on their own, but may become detectable in the presence of other components or groups of components. Though a fair number of effects are known, it seems unlikely that chemistry alone will ever be able to produce adequate descriptions of the flavour of malt whisky.

However, correlations can be established between specific compounds and taste. The galloyl esters mentioned in the table on page 163 are indicative of the presence of compounds which are associated with immaturity, while other compounds such as aromatic aldehydes are associated with the pleasanter tastes which come as the spirit matures.

Knowing which compounds produce particular tastes is one thing; ensuring that they occur is quite another. Since the lengthy maturation process imposes considerable costs on the distiller, much effort has gone into trying to accelerate the process and control the chemical changes that take place within the cask. But so complex are those changes that, for the foreseeable future, it seems likely that the most economical and convenient way of ensuring that whisky matures to perfection will be the simple one which our forebears discovered. You make a good malt spirit, you fill it into a good oak cask, and you wait for 10 or 20 years.

It is notable that there exists no popular equivalent of the whisky-tasting vocabulary which has been developed by the whisky industry, and that that vocabulary is of fairly recent origin. The reasons are not hard to find: until the 19th century, whisky was mostly made locally in small quantities and drunk immature by people who were not gentlemen. The whisky which was elevated to the status of a drink for the upper classes at the end of the century was blended whisky and it was taken with ice and soda. It isn't too surprising that there was no pressing need for a language with which to express nuances of flavour.

One of the advantages of blended whisky over malt, from a marketing point of view, was that it was possible to produce an absolutely uniform product, so that a given brand would taste the same from one year to the next and from one end of the world to the other. There was no need for a language, save to describe the differences among blends. That no such popular language evolved is perhaps surprising; maybe because the social *milieu* of whisky drinking tended to encourage allegiance to one brand rather than the sort of catholicity of taste which would encourage comparison. However that may be, the fact is that until relatively recently, there has been no accepted and available vocabulary for describing whisky.

There have been social barriers. MacDiarmid's dour drinker is not the sort of man who would be likely to wax lyrical about his dram. Indeed there is a strain in traditional Scottish male society which is deeply suspicious of any such activity and rates taciturnity one of the signs of manhood. There is good and bad in this: the pubs which MacDiarmid describes were awful places, not remotely like the pubs in which he actually did his drinking. In fact the society which he cultivated was far from dour, and the pubs in which he met his literary pals were renowned for the quality and quantity of the conversation. The good lay not in moroseness as such, so much as in its propensity to deflate pretension.

Curiously, the Scotland of the dreich Glasgow pub was also a land rich in song and story. If some of the stories tended to glorify dreich pubs with rules of silence, that was a contradiction to be savoured by connoisseurs of illogic. It was to be savoured in those houses which were islands of conviviality in a sea of moroseness. Places like Sandy Bell's and the Hebrides in Edinburgh, and the Scotia and the Victoria in Glasgow are still refuges, but from lounge bars with television and piped muzak. There are more of the former now, though, and the drink is infinitely better. You can get a decent beer in many pubs and malt whisky in most, so things are on the up. And it is no longer inconceivable that a Scottish man who is not actually homosexual should talk in public about the taste of his drink. (Lest anybody give me a hard time about the exclusively male reference, and my adverting to homosexuality, it should be borne in mind that we are talking about how things were and are, and about a society whose self-image was and is closely allied to its conception of masculinity.)

In recent years things have changed to a point at which we can both get a good drink and feel free to talk about it. The only problem is that we don't have an adequate vocabulary to talk about it with, much as desert dwellers don't have a lot of words for fish. The lack of terminology was a problem which faced us at the Scotch Malt Whisky Society, for we had to describe to our members (who were at a distance) what the stuff tasted like. And because we were bottling malt whiskies from single casks, each of which was highly individual in its flavours, the problem was especially severe.

We also had the problem that any descriptions had to be put in print, and not be impossibly boring. The sort of vocabulary which Russell Sharp describes as having been devised within the whisky industry for the identification of flavours is no doubt useful for the purposes for which it was devised. It makes pretty tedious reading. One possibility was the adoption *in toto* of the wine taster's vocabulary. This suffered from two difficulties: firstly, there are still remnants in most of us of the dour drinker syndrome and the flights of the (mostly southern English) wine taster's vocabulary were likely to stick in the craw; the second impediment was more serious: wine-tasting terms have been devised for describing wine. Whisky tastes different from wine; so many terms will not apply, and where they do, there may well be confusion.

There was (and is) a further difficulty with wine tasters'

language: it is largely inaccessible without a lengthy apprenticeship. Since the great majority of the people whom we hoped to attract to our new-found land of single-cask malts would be new to the stuff, there was going to be a translation problem. Some tasting terms can have an ostensible reference; if a person has tasted blackcurrants, he or she will know what you mean when you describe a whisky as tasting of blackcurrants. But many of the words in common use to describe wines are metaphors and pretty inaccessible. No doubt when the terms were coined, the metaphors were fresh and carried highly significant associations. But all metaphors have a life span, sometimes a brief one, and if they haven't acquired a new meaning by the end of it, they are worse than useless. It is one of the problems of subjective description that it sometimes isn't too easy to know whether a word still has any meaning or not, for to different people the metaphor will appear to be at different stages in its life cycle.

We decided that for all these reasons it would be best to ignore what had gone before and to do it from scratch. We had to create the language we required, or rather to adapt plain English, but in a way that would allow most reasonably sensible people to gain access. Fortunately, we had the machinery ready to hand. If you want to get people to generate descriptions of anything, there are few methods so reliable as sitting them down in front of a few bottles of really good malt and asking them to talk about it. How much more efficacious when the thing they are discussing is the malt itself!

Hence the Scotch Malt Whisky Society tasting committee, whose onerous task it is to taste all of the makes which the Society bottles and, while drinking the stuff, to talk about it. Out of the chat arise the ideas which are later converted into tasting notes, examples of which follow. It is our experience that ideas flow more freely after a few glasses and that, provided a certain order is maintained, the discussion does not stray too far from the point.

The qualifications for membership of the committee have never been defined, though literacy and a liking for the cratur are definitely required. You have to be able to think on your feet, so to speak. Mainly, you have to have been in the right place at the right time. The committee is largely self-selecting: alas, the pool of volunteers is so large that the only way of achieving any sort of fairness and equality is to satisfy none. There is, however, nothing to stop people doing it for themselves and, to that end, I offer a few hints on how to go about tasting malt whiskies. Remember, none of this is exactly serious; it doesn't really matter if you don't get it right; indeed in a thing as subjective as taste, there is no absolute right and wrong.

Three things are needed: whisky, water and glasses. The whisky goes without saying, though beginners would be well advised to choose spirits possessing marked rather than subtle characteristics. The water should be good, still water, having as little taste of its own as possible. There is no need to buy bottled water if decent tap water is to be had. (When holding whisky tastings, as the Society does around the country, the first thing we do is to taste the local water. It is surprising how with a little practice one can come to be discerning about something which previously one had taken entirely for granted.) Our experience is that you need a lot of water; much more than the whisky by volume.

Glasses are the subject of much dispute, but there is really no argument. You need a tasting glass that you can swirl the stuff around in and which has a fairly narrow neck to retain the vapours which give the nose. A copita is best, but a small brandy glass is good enough. The traditional whisky glass, the cut-crystal tumbler with the wide neck and tapering sides, is quite useless. It was devised in the 19th century and was for drinking blended whisky out of. Since the whisky was being mixed with ice and soda it had no nose to speak of.

The method of tasting is another matter about which we get a lot of dispute, mainly as regards the strength at which the whisky should be drunk. It is undoubtedly possible to drink malt whisky neat at 114 proof, but only if it is taken in such tiny quantities that the saliva dilutes the spirit. If you take it in any greater quantity, it will obliterate the palate and render you incapable of tasting anything for quite some time. (It may be that you are someone who is incapable of tasting anything anyway, in which case it won't matter.) There are still a few men around who think that it is demeaning to their masculinity to take a drop of water, on the ground that real men drink their whisky straight. Ernest Hemingway seems to have had a lot to do with this. There are two things everyone should know about Hemingway: that the whisky he drank straight was 70 proof, having been diluted substantially by the distillers before he got it; secondly, that the man was an awful fool.

Having assembled the necessary implements, three further elements are required: assiduous attention, plenty of practice and a certain humility. Taste can be trained, as can the other senses. If you want to learn badly enough, learn you will, but only if you know when you don't know. (That is where the humility comes in.) Put a little of the stuff in the glass, swirl it around, stick your snout in the hole and sniff. Do that a few times and then put water to it. Usually about as much water as whisky. Snout and sniff again. It is astonishing how the nose changes with the water, and often how it alters over time. We often find that after we have tasted a number of whiskies, it is worth going back over the glasses and nosing again, for the odours change dramatically over time. One could in theory spend an agreeable evening merely sniffing.

In the hope that readers may gain as much pleasure from tasting whisky as we have done, we offer a selection of the Society's tasting notes. The notes are not meant to be definitive; they are our observations and make no pretence of objectivity. They represent the joint subjectivity of our tasting panel and though we generally agree about most whiskies, we do occasionally find that one of the group, for no apparent reason, disagrees with his colleagues. We are not entirely sure how to regard this, but undoubtedly it happens and we feel that it is probably a good thing.

Scotch malt whiskies are usually classified by region: Highland, Island and Lowland. In addition to these, we have a few subdivisions. The Highland whiskies we would class as Northern, Eastern, Western and Perthshire. Speyside is a separate category and within that we would distinguish whiskies from the Findhorn, the Lossie, the Spey and the Deveron. Island whiskies we generally divide into Islay whiskies and the other islands, and Campbeltown is given a class of its own.

Taking the Scotch Malt Whisky Society whiskies in no particular order other than alphabetical (we have an arcane identification system which it is no part of this book to describe), some of our descriptions have been as follows. In some cases I have given two descriptions, to show the difference between casks of different kinds.

ABERLOUR

Golden in colour, it has a winey, cedar wood, vanilla syrupy-smooth aroma. It has a lovely flowery, malty flavour with a very slight peatiness – an intriguing, subtle dram worthy of repetitive tastings.

ARDBEG

A fine gold colour; second-fill sherry cask. There are lots of odours besides the peat: yeast, malt, iodine and seaweed as well as something reminiscent of flowers on the machar. Sweet taste and dry aftertaste. This is as good as it gets.

AUCHENTOSHAN

This whisky is almost colourless, from a plain oak cask. Water elicits peardrops in the nose, with a hint of vanilla. The theme is repeated in the taste, which is very curious; mild and reminiscent of custard puddings. This is a most unusual whisky and good once you make the necessary adjustment. It is a local character and shows the range of which the stuff is capable. The best we have had from this distillery.

BALMENACH

The whisky in this bottling is pale-coloured, with a strong, striking nose which is at odds with the mainly sweet taste. Complicated: a gustatory dialectic in which the antithesis of the taste meets the thesis of the nose to produce a satisfying synthesis of sensation.

BALVENIE

Golden-coloured, with a vast range of flavours including grass, peardrop and floral notes together with a toffee/ butterscotch taste. Typical of a first-class bourbon cask.

BENRINNES

This bottling is from a first-fill cask of sweet sherry. The whisky is as dark as rum; the colour – and a hint of the taste – of stewed prunes. An after-supper drink.

BENROMACH

Although sadly now closed, this distillery long enjoyed a high reputation for the excellence of its product. This cask has given a pale golden colour; the whisky is sweet without being cloying. It has a fresh flavour of cut barley.

BLADNOCH

Golden in colour, it has an estery, fruity, citrusy aroma and a delicate, smooth flavour – a memorable dram.

BOWMORE

A complex, peaty whisky with a nose-warming, astringent aroma. This dram has a robust flavour with shades of iodine, sweet notes and an exceptional aftertaste.

BRUICHLADDICH

This is kindly stuff and one of the mildest-tasting of Islay whiskies. It has a strong nose with no hint of peat until you add water. It is flowery in taste for an Island malt; not heavily peated and having a hint of sea water.

BUNNAHABHAIN

A butter toffee colour; from a sherry butt, this has a big nose, redolent of grappa or marc; at the brandy end of the spectrum. Like a Speyside at the start, it is an Islay on the aftertaste; an Islay for those who don't like Island whiskies.

BUSHMILLS

Pale gold in colour, smooth on the palate, syrupy.

CAOL ILA

Pale gold in colour, with a pronounced peaty, crushed-barley aroma. It is evident from the nose alone that this is an Island whisky and it has in full measure those qualities so valued by lovers of the genre. The peat dominates but does not diminish the other flavours: there are lots of them there, but what they are, it's hard to say. Pastel-coloured tastes, compared with the peaty primary. Very dry.

COLEBURN

Almost nine years in a good sherry butt has given a fine dark colour while leaving the spirit very strong. The nose is perfectly balanced between peat and sweetness. The whisky can take a lot of water, which elicits a leafy, privet sort of smell. On the tongue it is quite sharp: it is complex, and successive layers reveal themselves with time. It would make fine Atholl Brose.

CRAGGANMORE

The whisky is from dark sherry wood. It looks and smells not unlike a tawny port. It is rich and winey, probably the first fill of an oloroso cask. It is old – 18 years in the wood – but there is no trace of the woodiness which so often spoils older whiskies. It has the colour and the closeness of texture of Honduras mahogany. Take it with water but don't drown it, for it is a liqueur whisky if ever there was.

DALLAS DHU

First cask: The pale colour of this whisky, from a plain oak cask, contrasts strongly with some of our earlier casks of the same. The oak comes over in the nose and the woody theme is repeated in the taste, but more aromatically; cedar and dailuaine cinnamon rather than oak and tannin. A good dram, subtle but straightforward.

Second cask: A good whisky hitherto used entirely for blending. This cask has produced a peculiar, greenish colour, probably the result of high iron content. Because of the colour, we were apprehensive about offering this cask, but we tried the whisky out on members who happened to be visiting Leith and, since the members who tasted it were unanimously in favour, we decided to bottle it. Toffee nose, it improves chromatically and gastronomically with water. A taste of caramel but quite dry.

DALMORE

Pale colour, from a plain oak, or maybe a bourbon cask, it has a high flowery nose. On the palate, it is reminiscent of elderflower wine, or vanilla pods in sugar. A big, complex whisky. Definitely not for amateurs.

GLENDEVERON

First cask: A good sherry cask has given the spirit a rich, golden colour. The nose is redolent of fruit and caramel – toffee apples and a touch of candy peel. The taste is both sweet and sharp. A distinctive dram which will reward time spent in the drinking (this for the puritans among you, who feel the need of a utilitarian justification).

Second cask: This is a perfectly pale spirit from a plain oak cask, yet it has a sweet, substantial, oleaginous nose. There is a hint of menthol with water; a sweet, sugar-fudge taste and an aftertaste of honey. This shows that the roundness and sweetness of a really good Speyside does not depend on sherry wood. Don't use too much water with it: its characteristics are more apparent when taken quite strong.

GLENFARCLAS
A rich, sherry wood colour and aroma: honey, caramel, rosewater present themselves to the nose – and, in turn, to the palate. A remarkably mature whisky given its relative youth, it demonstrates what we have long been saying, namely that it is the quality of the cask that counts and not (beyond a certain lower limit) the length of time in wood.

GLENFIDDICH
A pale, blond colour, light, unobtrusive nose; this whisky has manners suitable for the airport lounges where it is commonly found. It is well bred, well balanced, unostentatious and safe. Good, too.

GLEN GARIOCH
Peaty and grassy with a robust flavour. This is a fine example of a traditional whisky which has been well matured in remade hogsheads. Pale golden in colour.

GLENGLASSAUGH
A superb dram, normally used only for blending. Rich, smooth, cognac-like.

GLEN GRANT
A golden colour; a big, robust whisky, with a slightly sweet, peaty, malty flavour. An after-dinner dram.

GLENLIVET
First cask: Pale colour from a Limousin oak cask. Nose of damp oak woods, woody Spanish wines: it changes

prodigiously with water to yield coconuts, vanilla pods, peardrops, changing all the time. The taste is all you might expect from such a cask.

Second cask: A darker cask, sherry wood, but old: smells like a warehouse, mould at a distance. The nose again comes out with water. Don't even think of drinking this straight, but take it with a fair drop. It can stand it. Fruity taste, with a hint of Calvados, among a dozen or so other things, few of which we could place – but then we didn't spend all night, as you may wish to.

GLENLOSSIE
This cask has given a deep, dark colour so that even after a judicious addition of water, the whisky is still darker than a tawny sherry. Don't use a lot of water on it, though. This is one of the sweetest whiskies we have bottled and is to be taken as a dessert rather than as an aperitif.

GLEN TURRET
This bottling is from a bourbon cask. Its nose has the floweriness which is characteristic of such; it opens up with water and yields scents of elderflower and Liebfraumilch. It is entirely honest, not appearing to be anything it isn't, but what it is, is sufficient: an entirely pleasing and agreeable whisky.

HIGHLAND PARK
Dark red colour, from the first filling of an oloroso cask. The sherry comes over on the nose, sweet and rich. It tastes of cedar and peaches, but with a dry aftertaste which makes you want to go back for more. This is a post-prandial whisky. Keep it in the glass and the taste will

develop with time. David says it is a conversation whisky: it both stimulates the conversation and takes part in it.

INCHGOWER

Gold in colour, it has a slightly grainy, barley, cut-grass, malty aroma. It has a light, satisfying, well-balanced flavour.

INVERLEVEN

This is undoubtedly one of the finest Lowland malts but alas the still which produced it has been decommissioned, so that supplies are finite. From a second-fill sherry cask which has given a good golden colour, the whisky has a buttery nose which holds up well when watered. The taste is sweet; it clings like toffee.

ISLE OF JURA

Pale golden in colour, with a soft, peaty, fragrant, delicate aroma and a beautifully smooth, sweet, vanilla flavour. The characteristics of this whisky are those more properly associated with Island whiskies than the peatiness for which they are best known. It is salty and oily, as with some of the Campbeltowns.

LAPHROAIG

Golden coloured; a highly peated aroma in a balanced combination with the malty, floral, vanilla flavour.

LEDAIG

First cask: The whisky is lightly peated for an Island malt: an Island whisky for those whose preference generally runs to other things. Dark gold colour from a good sherry cask and a smell of violets. A good introduction to Island whiskies, it has peat and sweetness too: old-fashioned humbugs or bog boilings, if your imagination will stretch that far. Cinnamon and spice, peaty but not medicinal. An Island whisky for dwellers in a semi rather than a blackhouse.

Second cask: The spirit is very pale, from a plain oak cask. The colour leaves one unprepared for the astonishing saddleroom, leathery smell, which is presumably a variety of peatiness. Most intriguing. Someone said it has a stereo nose, one smell up one nostril and one up the other. Sweet tasting, it is very easy to come to terms with, so don't be put off by the foregoing.

LINKWOOD
The whisky has a fine, dark colour, from the second fill of a good sherry cask. The nose does not belie the appearance and the taste is sweet, with toffee and caramel. The aftertaste has something we couldn't place, maybe citrus or cut barley. A sipping whisky.

LONGMORN–GLENLIVET
This whisky is toffee-nosed but democratic, sophisticated and understated. Sweet, aromatic, with odours of liquorice, caraway and flowering currant. This is not for beginners, on whom it would be wasted. Keep it to yourself, or give drams to the cognoscenti. It isn't cheap, but then the best never is.

MACALLAN
Known for its reputation as having been aged in fine sherry wood, this whisky needs no introduction to members. A light nose, which do not disregard; it repays attention. There is more body than the colour suggests, for this is not one of your second- or third-fill casks. Drink a chilled manzanilla before, this after.

PORT ELLEN

Rich gold in colour, this whisky has a superb aroma: a mix of peatiness, caramel, vanilla and raisins. The product of a faultless maturation in a cask of exceptional quality. The vanilla, oak, syrupy flavours in perfect balance with the distinctive peatiness and distillate flavours provide a uniquely desirable experience.

PULTENEY

This bottling is golden in colour with a very zesty refreshing aroma with a hint of peat. It has a wonderful oaky, vanilla flavour that is beyond description but must be savoured.

ROSEBANK

The whisky has a dark red colour, from the first fill of an oloroso cask. We don't get many Lowland whiskies of such provenance. The nose is much more pungent than you would expect from sherry-cask whisky; it ameliorates and sweetens with water. A sweet, robust taste. This is an uncomplicated, brandy-like whisky for taking after dinner.

ROYAL BRACKLA

Pale gold, this is slightly peaty, with a cut-barley, grassy aroma. Exceptionally smooth and mellow with a slightly winey, raisiny flavour.

SCAPA

This bottling is the colour of new-sawn oak. An immensely complex nose: pungent herbs – thyme, bayleaf, bog myrtle – sweet shops of one's childhood: peardrops, old-fashioned humbugs. A rich, full taste, is one for the hip flask and the open air of a Highland morning.

SPRINGBANK

First cask: Dark gold colour, very raisiny and sherried with an appetisingly rich flavour. A marvellous balance between the whisky and the sherry wood has produced an excellent post-prandial dram.

Second cask: A golden-coloured dram, matured in an amontillado cask. Floral, cut-grass, vanilla notes subtly sherried harmonise gently, resulting in a wonderful whisky with a fresh flavour.

Third cask: Unmistakable, complex nose; medium sweet sherry with pepper, raisins, allspice, vanilla. Dark gold colour, rich taste, slight sourness, sulphur and that classic malt smell. A black bun of a whisky.

ST MAGDALENE

From the now-closed Linlithgow distillery. Bijou flats where once the barley brewed, alas. The whisky pale, lemon-coloured, from an oak cask. Sweet and dry at the same time; a hint of lemon balm underlying a caramel flavour. A long, dry aftertaste. A good, traditional dram.

TAMDHU

Rich, dark gold, indicating its sherry-cask maturation. With a distinct sherry aroma – full of fruit, with oak and cedar wood characteristics, it is redolent of the maturing warehouse. It has a superbly mellow smoothness of flavour for such a big, complex whisky – definitely one for winter nights with a few close friends.

TAMNAVOULIN

Pale gold from an oak cask, this is another of the very best. The nose responds well to patience, giving scents of the haystack and damp barley which with water are transformed to a clean, sweet odour. The taste shows that John Barleycorn did not die in vain.

TOMATIN

One of the largest distilleries in the Highlands with very pure water drawn from the local burn. These factors go towards making the distinctive taste. Golden in colour, this has a fruity, slightly caramel, oaky aroma. It has a very smooth and interesting flavour – this is an excellent dram from a very underrated distillery.